My Life in Ladies' Knickers

OSCAR SPARROW

Copyright © 2019 Oscar Sparrow
All rights reserved.
ISBN: 9781916097575

All rights reserved. No part of this book may be reproduced or transmitted in any form or by any means, electronic or mechanical, including photocopying, recording, or any information storage and retrieval system, without prior written permission of the author. Your support of the author's rights is appreciated.
All characters in this compilation are fictitious. Any resemblance to actual persons, living or dead, is purely coincidental.

DEDICATION

To all you guys who suck it up.

CONTENTS

A Note From Oscar	Pg 1
Introduction – Lifting The Drain Cover	Pg 3
Chapter One – Chapter Twenty-nine	Pg 7-187
Epilogue	Pg 188
A Message From Oscar	Pg 191
Free Book	Pg 193
More Books by Oscar Sparrow	Pg 195
Handy Resource Guide For Writers	Pg 201
About Oscar Sparrow	Pg 203
Find Oscar Sparrow Online	Pg 205
Publisher	Pg 207

A NOTE FROM OSCAR

I am an English author and regret I have not had the education in life to write the superior form of English that is spoken in the USA.

INTRODUCTION—LIFTING THE DRAIN COVER

I was born with a severely nibbled X-chromosome. I've just had to play the hand I received and suck it up. I've never applied for a special parking permit or counselling. Many liberal governments are now beginning to introduce remedial therapies and there are hopes for a complete cure but it has all come too late for me.

I find women very attractive and although I know it's wrong, I can't stop myself. As a proud male I don't read book introductions or television installation instructions. If I end up not understanding what I'm reading or watching a fuzzy black and white picture that's fine cos that's the way I wanted it all along.

Dude—the solution is in your hands. Ladies, I know you're reading this. The *mansplaining* is for that thick idle bastard snoring on the sofa. Be gentle—he's a mutant and can't help it.

This is a self-help manual and such books **require a lot of bold text.** It is also a tender and heart-sucking romantic comedy based around the worlds of sewage management and English Literature.

If like me you are, or are planning to be, a rejected misunderstood artistic genius, or have ever sat on or flushed a toilet, this book is for you.

It's the true story of a fifty-seven-year-old guy who finds himself driving a sewage tanker for a living and with little to show for his life. This stinking outcast goes on to be a best-selling *'female'* romantic novelist. He did this…

…because he wanted to achieve that goal.

Now, can you find those last three words in your heart? For the moment forget characterization, story arcs, sub plots and all the stuff that goes into books. You can learn all that technique as you develop. Relax and come with me while I reveal how you can use life's smacks in the gob to get yourself off the floor, stand erect as a man **and go on to be a winner.**

In my other identity I'm a major romance writer with thousands of sincere fans throughout the world. In fairness and respect for my readers I cannot reveal my true name and destroy their dreams. Titles of books have been changed and locations shifted. Professional writers' groups have been re-named in order to protect other sincere and talented writers. I live in awe and admiration of many literary professionals who bring joy to their readers. Occasionally we rub shoulders even though they do not know my identity or catch any whiff of my history.

This is a true, sexy, dramatic and violent story, yet no romantic novelists or sewage operatives were harmed in the writing of this book.

If you wanted a self-help book with bullet points and trite motivational sayings, you've been cheated, or you've pushed the wrong button. I hope you can still get your money back. I'm an entirely self-uneducated guy—no university, no creative writing diplomas. Self-help books have helped me a lot with technical know-how of writing mechanics. All the same, is it useful if some guru says,

> **"There's no reverse gear on a moon rocket"**
> or
> **"Your courage is hiding in the guy you're afraid to be."**?

I just made up that rubbish to show off. You could make up that stuff all day yourselves, so you don't need me. Hey—your self-help book will probably sell more than mine. I'll leave a couple of blank pages in the book for you to record your own aphorisms. (OK–I didn't know what it meant until I looked it up).

This is a motivational book in the real sense. It's about a man who dreams of being a writer but it could apply to any situation. Our connected Internet society puts big-biz power in your hands. We live in the context of cars that won't start, kids who think you're stupid, kids who are often right about you, rents you can't pay, would-be partners you long for but can't attract, jobs you hate, *snides* who slap you down and bus drivers who saw you running and floored the pedal. This shitty frustrating existence is the tragicomedy we need to understand and then overcome.

You will see sections in **bold type** where I hold the narrative briefly in order to give some tip or insight. Finally, you'll note, I often refer to you guys as *comrades*. This does not imply any political attitude. You're my comrades because we're fighting our way off the floor. The same boots have kicked us up the ass, the same rejections have put us down, the same desire burns in our hearts. If you're going to come further with me now, you'll never be less than my comrade. I am Oscar Sparrow, the official Poet Lorry-Park.

1 CHAPTER ONE

The swallows have gone and a few fallen leaves swirl at my feet. The golden harvest is in and the starlings chatter, whistle and click their anthem to autumn. The sky is a thin pale blue while the air carries a smoky edge of wistful sadness, still playing a remembered tune of lust, love and noble sorrow to store in the soul for winter.

All in all, a good day to rip off my lacy gusset and get into some nice clean Y-fronts and talk about the best-selling author inside all of us. I'm sorry about the opening. Perhaps you thought you'd picked up a soppy romance by mistake? In a certain sense you have but let me tell you how it all began.

By inclination I'm a poet. By trade I'm a sewage worker. In general, this is not the natural apprenticeship for a career in literature. My job is to drive an effluent tanker truck. You may have seen such vehicles, dribbling liquid from an anus-type valve at the rear. Very often the trucks are muddy and smeared with excrement. Commonly so are the drivers but the anal dribbling still lies ahead on my career path. The work involves sucking out cess-pits or septic tanks, emptying ships' bilges and the clearing of drains, sewers and gulleys. (My mate Donald Trump uses the expression *shitholes*. Although we've never met, Don is my good friend and if you read on you will learn how he diverted the American fleet to save me.) On some days I drive solid waste away from sewage treatment plants for distribution on agricultural land. Other days I drive tons of stinking food waste to land fill tips.

When someone tells you their life is shit, believe me, it probably is not. My life *is* shit and, in many ways, I love it. All of my activities allow time for contemplation. Often, I have to queue to pump off three thousand gallons of untreated animal urine or human foul water containing turds and used condoms. Generally, I read self-improvement books and listen to the BBC Radio 4 channel where educated people talk about politics, art, literature, cuisine, economics and many things far too clever for me to understand. It was while sucking out a blocked abattoir sludge sump that a radio show changed my life.

A lady from the famous Frills and Spoons publishing house was talking about romance books. Apparently, they were desperate to hear from exciting new writers—people who had a fresh and unique viewpoint on the affairs of humanity. That just had to be me. For Christ's sake—why hadn't I seen it before? I didn't have to pass the rest of my life as an untouchable. I already knew the visceral power of appetite and passion from the bowel end.

Just then the suction hose started to buck and thrash in its customary orgasmic spasm as the sump dregs mixed with air. Often this is an almost Wagnerian moment of climax—the *Fart of the Valkyries* or what I call the *Gotterdamerdung*. I shut down the vacuum pump and extracted my hard, six-inch end-pipe from the slimy hole. My friends, I knew in that moment that I had always been destined to be a romantic novelist. And what is a writer? A writer is someone who writes. Romantic stories swarmed into my mind from my own worship at the perfumed shrine of womanhood. I needed a blank sheet of paper and a brain dump.

I pumped out my load at the municipal treatment plant and drove the tanker to the local ASDA store. The sewage worker often faces social humiliation. Shit-smeared stinking clothing can block many social connections. Think of it as being a state of reverse-polarity celebrity. One is rarely in a crowd. I made my way to the books department and studied the Frills and Spoons romance display. Almost at random I purchased four titles and added a couple of school-style exercise books and a pack of cheap ball point pens. I added a budget extra-large sausage roll and queued at the check-out. A glance at one of the books entitled *Claiming His Pregnant Wife*, informed me that a guy called Francesco Romanelli was fighting to contain his molten outrage. No such emotion had ever swept over me. There was going to be a lot to learn.

The young lady on the till tried not to look at me. She was pretty but with severely hacked blue and pink hair and spoke with a foreign accent. I guessed that few middle-aged guys in overalls bought romance books but I figured it might be a conversation opener.

"Do you read these?"

"No."

"Me neither, but I'm going to start."

"Why?"

"Why does anyone read books?"

"I don't know."

The poor child was trying not to inhale but knowing the market was a vital element of the business. The lady on the radio had stressed that one just had to connect with one's readers. I'd made a start.

I withdrew to my truck, wiped off my hands and set about the sausage roll. I opened another of the books *The Italian Billionaire's Secret Love Child.* A handsome rich male called Ricardo di Napoli was consorting with an even more gorgeous but poor woman. Suddenly I was in a different world of sports cars and luxury yachts with a sprinkling of unexpected babies. No longer was I a stinking social outcast eating cheap junk food in a foul diesel-fuel-scented truck cab. I had taken my first steps toward fame and honours. Romance seemed to be anything but real. I imagined myself tanned and tall at the wheel of my Ferrari. I thought of the lady on the radio longing to hear new fresh voices. A writer is someone who *writes* and I was on my way to fill her longing. Within a few minutes I was asleep. I'd had a very, very bad night. Beyond the superficial glamour of my artistic life, my existence lay in ruins. All will become clear.

The ASDA parking guy was hammering on my cab door.

"Get this stinking thing out of here. You're blocking eight slots. No trucks—can't you read?"

I wound down the window and waved a book at him.

"Not only do I read but I'm a trainee romantic novelist."

"Fuck off or the manager's going to call the police."

"A man is never a prophet in his own shit-hole."

"Just fuck off."

I smiled gently, as if I were a refined novelist or maybe even Ricardo di Napoli and started the engine. Even so at that moment my new life had begun. I had come out. On posh BBC radio, arty people were always talking about coming out. I had had my Epiphany. I checked my work sheet. It was a highly aromatic suck-out of pig waste slurry but not even that could dent my dream. That fine lady had wanted fresh new voices and I was on my way to whisper into the gorgeous folds of her bejewelled perfumed ear.

2 CHAPTER TWO

That evening I slumped down in my underwear on my bed in my seedy rented room. The house was let out in single cells by the entrepreneurial Mr. Singh. Other residents had asked me to leave my outer clothing in the garden. For the sake of peace and good manners I complied.

I spread out my books and examined the titles. There was *Claiming His Pregnant Wife, The Mediterranean Millionaire's Reluctant Mistress, The Frenchman's Demand* and *Millionaire to the Rescue.*

I opened a book to read. It was only a few seconds later that a house brick smashed through the window. Oh no! My literary career would have to stay on hold for a while.

There's a reason for everything. Bricks arriving through my window were not entirely unexpected. Such events were one of the stepping-stones which led to my life in ladies' knickers. This is a book about the publishing business and for anyone interested in writing a book. It is also a true story about the nightmare of stalking which happened to coincide with my life as the romantic novelist, Michelle Mabelle. Please, do bear with me and everything will become clear.

I have always been a poet and a writer. I have been rejected by the greatest publishers, agents and editors in the business. Trust me comrades when I say that the first forty years of wall to wall rejections are the worst. If you're still writing and learning—you're a writer. Few of the GREATS have trodden your path. None of the GREATS write like you. I'll come back to this subject later.

A useful lump of concrete skittled my electric kettle across the floor. My Pot Noodle dinner feast would have to wait. I looked out of the window and saw a woman of about fifty-five years. She pulled up her skirt to reveal her naked pubis. She pointed to her genitals and shrieked.

"Fuck you. Fuck you. Don't you want some of this you bastard? You prick—you could have me!"

I watched her bend down and select another half-brick from a pile at her feet. She threw wildly and smashed the front door. I wondered if this is the kind of molten passion that goes on around Ricardo di Napoli? She threw again and hit the front upstairs room where four or five Polish guys lived. I heard them thunder out onto the landing like a swarm of Slavic killer-wasps. They crashed down the stairs and hammered at my door. The voice was that of a superman builder called Kaz.

"Oscar—you are crazy man. She break the fucking window. Go out and give her your cock. She doesn't want much."

"Don't insult my cock," I replied in an attempt at insouciant suavity.

"Give her cock or we kill you."

"You give her your cock."

"She is horrible old woman. You old Oscar, your cock is right for her."

I liked Kaz. He was a grafter working as a night club bouncer and on building sites. His dream was to become a professional cage fighter with his stage name of Kruncher Krakow. There was the sound of more breaking glass as the remains of my front window took another hit. Suddenly there were blue police-lights. I watched as my admirer struggled with a couple of officers. I found the courage to open the door and pushed my way through a crowd of Polish guys, a black guy called Lulu who was smoking a joint and a Hell's Angel who everyone knew as Spike on account of his Mad Max Mohican hair style.

Still in my underwear, I emerged into public view as the police were loading the woman into a van. She looked up and saw me. Her eyes were swollen and mascara smeared her cheeks.

"I fucking love you!" she screamed as the officers slammed the doors.

If I was to become a romantic novelist, I knew I needed to savour this moment. Could Ricardo di Napoli or Francesco Romanelli have drawn such passion from the heart of a woman? Wow—how that lady from Frills and Spoons would love this story.

3 CHAPTER THREE

Fellow writers, comrade poets, you instinctively know my struggle with life. I feel safe and able to open my heart to you guys of all sexes and the increasing number hovering between the four or five established gender groups. My life had not been a success in personal or artistic terms. When I had a proper home of my own, publishers' rejection letters were the only wallpaper I could afford. Several incidents of unanticipated unilateral bin bagging had led to my residence in the rented room chez Mr. Singh.
    It is a fact that I have a profound, reckless and courageous weakness for women. That emotional symphony, that luscious joy of soft absorption that starts in selfless passion, then queues to park on match-day Saturdays in IKEA and ends in passive financial castration by Amazon. Please read to the end of this self-help book but the following is the greatest truth a poet can impart.

If your life hasn't been an humiliating dangerous experiment you never truly wanted to discover anything.

    OK, my admirer had been carted away by the police. A fine lady-constable of the Southleigh Constabulary had joined me in my superbly ventilated one-room abode. As I taped cardboard to the gaping hole, I had the chance to assess her beauty. She was young—maybe forty. She was a size eighteen, had dark hair in a bun and white teeth that crossed slightly, in order to soften the unapproachable perfection most women possess. The shrewdness in her dark eyes couldn't hide their kindness. Her full plump lips oozed warmth and tenderness. And this goddess was seated on my bed. She opened conversation with that ageless put down to an old zygote exposing his one-legged X chromosome.

"Maybe you'd be more comfortable with some clothes on."

"I would have dressed but I didn't know you were coming. I have to take my clothes off in the garden you see."

She smiled in that humouring way official people have when they're not sure if you're the sort of person who writes hate mail in green ink.

"Is there a reason for that?"

"There's a reason for everything. Basically, I smell bad."

I could tell the poor woman was raking through the police manual of diplomacy to compose the next sentence. I took pity.

"I'm a sewage tanker driver but a lot of local people know me as the Poet Lorry-Park."

"Laureate?"

"Lorry-Park for now. I'm waiting for a call from the palace. I'm also on the way to being a romantic novelist. Do you read that kind of thing?"

She glanced at the scattered books.

"Not really. The men are all kind of handsome dark heroes with big equipment. Most guys are more like you."

"Poets?"

"More like pale and poor."

"There was me thinking you liked me."

She smiled weakly while I selected an old track suit from one of the Tesco carrier bags which formed my wardrobe. A second carrier bag formed my larder of Fray Bentos tinned pies and cans of baked beans.

"OK, Oscar, tell me what the hell was going on out there?"

"It was a serious case of emotional overload. One sniff of me and some women lose their senses."

The gorgeous police angel shook her head, took out a wad of official paper and started to write.

Statement of Oscar Sparrow.
Born: 21.5.1949
Occupation: Lorry driver (Sewage)...

I am a member of the Southleigh Arts and Poetry Society. I was invited to join a few weeks ago after I won a poetry competition organised by the town council to celebrate multicultural diversity within the borough. I borrowed from the Bard Robbie Burns and wrote an *Address To A Kebab*. I was quite surprised to win but the other man did a rhyme called *Brown on White Love You Longtime*. It was about a Polish guy who'd been knocked over by a Sikh bus driver outside the Thai nail bar. The judges invited both of us into the elite circle of municipal art. That was how I met Betty Black.

She was already a leading member and quite often published her work in the poetry corner of the *Southleigh Shopper* free magazine. Maybe I should say that she is a very heavy smoker and you probably noticed she has the vocal chords of a strangled kipper. I had read an example of her work called *Swine*. I remember the lines—

Stuck pig.
No more porkies on my skewer,
Your chipolata excuse for sausage
on my hanging hook.
Punch and Judy sand in my crocodile sandwich.
That's the way to do it

I told her I'd found it redolent of childhood, clashing with the frustration of my adolescence. I admired its understated surrealism and quality of Dada-inspired automatic writings. In that moment I saw that Betty was a woman who had waited all her life for someone to appreciate her hidden depths.

My first impression was of an attractive woman with very dark eyes and something exotic in her nature. Her black hair seemed to have shot out of her head like electrocuted characters in comic strips. When she spoke, she added wild passionate hand movements, throwing back her head with artistic flourishes. I found myself watching the anger and compassion colliding in her wild psyche. I knew she knew I was watching her. She was like the dark bruise of a thunderstorm out to sea while you are still seated on a warm seductive sandy beach, wondering how long you can safely stay calm. It wasn't long before the first hot raindrop had me running for cover.

The police lady paused her writing and flexed her sans-ring beautiful hand.
"I can tell you're a poet, but can you keep things plain?"
"I'm sorry—we artists you understand—,"

Witness statement to police cont'd....

The day before yesterday I went to the next monthly meeting of the Arts Society. Betty was there, as was Colin Codbury, the official Bard of Southleigh. He'd just done an ode to the new waste incinerator which I recall—

Reversing beeps the night disturb as lorries nudge the concrete kerb.

He would expect you to know of him because he writes the odes to Southleigh United FC in the programme. He is professor of creative writing at the university. The format of the evening was that everyone read out their latest poem and the others offered praise or criticism. Betty presented a little piece entitled *Toast*. It went—

You scorch me thinking you can shoot me out
when time is up.
Boing boing you prick.
Feel my heat and scraping knife.
Take my citric acid spread
I'll drink to that.
Toast.

She delivered her poem with a magnificent force of anger and venom. For a moment there was silence. Colin Codbury was the first to speak.
"I don't think I would have used the term 'boing boing'. It lends a species of farcicality to an otherwise emotional first-person

accusative"

"Boing boing fucking boing, you bow-tied stuck-up twat. I'll boing over to you and give you a fucking first person in your face if you want one?" said Betty.

I must admit I was impressed. This was the first time in my fifty-seven years that I had met fellow poets and artists. It was at once clear that intercourse between sewage operatives was generally on a higher plain.

"I think the 'boing boing' captures and reflects the banality of what I call the logistics of passion. A poet can touch the infinity of joy with his beloved but in the light of day he has to defecate and put on his socks," I said.

"I'd defecate in his fucking socks," she commented.

"I noted on your competition entry that you are involved in excrement, Sparrow," said Codbury.

"I've been up to my eyes in it, sir, but I'm about to drown in it here by the look of it."

Betty shrieked and pounded the table.

"That's fucking smacked your gob Colin!"

The town laureate sneered with thin wet lips and read out his own effort. It was something about one of his students wondering if *zir* would be the personal pronoun for Mr. Darcy, if he were to go into gender transition.

"That Jane Austen was a money obsessed cock-sucker," said Betty.

I decided to offer some healing words.

"I think the poem rather raises the dilemma of contemporary uncertainty set against the tableau of enforced stereotyping in Austen's period."

"In a shallow obvious and untutored-sense, you begin to see the meaning," said Codbury.

Betty affected a throat clearing and spitting sound.

"In a shallow and obvious sense, you're a mega dick-head."

While other poets read out their work, I enjoyed the stimulating company of other artists. Several times I caught Betty's eyes on mine and to be honest I felt flattered and somehow validated. She was very attractive in a kind of feral way and to me she was the best poet in the room. Her work was straight from the gun into your forehead. Clearly, she shared my dislike for Codbury. Her aggressive disrespect for him shocked the natural sense of subservience in me which attaches to professional shit-suckers. She was smartly dressed in a business suit and wore quite extreme high heels. Her dark eyes were quick and alert. She was as bright and as dangerous as a stainless-steel blade. I'm a lover of the female mechanism but this one had an urgent red overload lamp flashing on the control panel.

The meeting took place in a room at the King Charles Arms. When it was over there was time to sink a couple of pints and it was then I made the mistake of my life.

"I could use a drink. You up for joining me?" she said.

I looked at her and I think I actually let out something between a sigh and a groan. I stared at the pulsing danger lamp somewhere in the area of her breasts. For the first time in my life I realised why sirens are called sirens.

"Yeah, Let's do it."

"Mine's a triple-whisky, with some ice."

While she went outside to demolish a full-strength Marlboro I set her up her drink and sat sipping a lager while she made her way to join me at a corner table.

"Thanks for your support. I've been watching you," she said.

Her voice was deep and smoky.

"How watching me?"

"You live quite near me. I saw your entry for the competition. I've sort of *selected* you."

"Selected—like a record on an old-fashioned juke box or something?"

"Juke box? What the hell are you? Are you stuck in some sort of geriatric time warp?"

"Not stuck but safely at anchor. I only just got a smart phone."

"Give me the number."

"Why?" I asked.

"Why not? We're poets and we share, like Van Gogh and Gaugin."

"Don't tell me—you're Van Gogh, right."

"Yeah—crazy mad genius."

"Not sure if I want to play Gaugin. Post Impressionism has always left me in a kind of pre-proto cubist void."

"Would you like to touch my pussy?" she asked, shrugging off my practised BBC Radio 4 intellectualism.

I must admit I blinked and may well have let my poetic jaw drop. The truth is that in my un-pussied life as an ageing, defiled, social outcast, this might be my last chance. She was clever, now even more desperately attractive but destructively mad.

"Were we not discussing Art?"

"Huh, I thought I might have met a man at last? You're just a limp fucking phallus like the rest. I thought you might want to worship in the hot lava juice of my shrine?"

"I do like that kind of thing, in a verified protestant shrine context," I replied.

"D'you smoke—you know *smoke*?"

"No, quite often there's methane in the sewers—it can be dangerous."

"You're thicker than that prick Colin Codbury. He smokes weed but doesn't inhale in case they find out at the Masonic lodge."

"You have been friends?"

"Not penetrative—he's got nothing."

"I think I'd be equally disappointing."

I watched her dark eyes flash across my face and then focus on the ceiling. Her jaw was clenched and angry.

"I'm trying to keep my patience with you, Sparrow. You're a little, little man who's been gifted a ticket to a higher level. You are nothing but a pot-bellied self-confessed turd-monkey. I hate, loathe and despise myself for having thought you attractive enough to humble and prostrate myself in front of you."

"You have a way with words Betty. I think the loathing and humbling should be strong enough in themselves. There's a degree of tautology in your verbal broadside," I said.

She fixed me with the kind of gaze that only someone like Ricardo Di Napoli could summon up.

"Don't get clever intelligent with me. You can stuff your tautology up your rectal anal ass-hole sphincter."

"You're quick," I said, actually enjoying the wild bucking danger of her. "What do you do in the world?"

"I waste my time on greedy thick business-types. I'm a corporate lawyer."

"That's impressive."

"I don't want some soft loser who's impressed by people."

"I wasn't making an application."

"I'll get you a drink," she said.

"Lager please."

"Fuck off. When I pay, I choose. You're only starting to understand what you've started."

I let out a lungful of air and watched her clack to the bar on her Madame Whiplash heels. She sure was all woman. Now was the time to head for the toilet and go out through the window. When she came back with a bottle of Cote du Rhone and whisky chasers I was still there.

The policewoman stood up and stretched her arm and shoulders.

"I could offer to give your poor neck a relaxing squeeze?" I said, not in total innocence.

"Thanks, but no thanks."

"I guess I'm too old."

"I know I'm too young."

"Would you like a glass of Aldi Merlot from my own cellars?"

"Mr. Sparrow, I really would like that," she said with a warm smile.

I poured half pint glasses of wine.

"You never quite know what will happen when you meet someone new do you?" I said.

She gave me an amused, appraising once over.

"Oscar, I think you're a bit disingenuous. You're a victim and maybe eventually you'll get state-certification as a survivor but deep down, you're a manipulative but harmless womanizer."

"I'd not really felt anything for a woman until I met you."

"You just can't help yourself, can you? How many times have you been bin-bagged?"

"Well, I'm still in single figures—just."

"A lot of folks live a whole a life without drama, violence, broken relationships and crazy stalkers."

"It's awful for them isn't it. You see I've lived what I now need to write. Everything has been about developing my craft and characterisation. I've been an unconscious victim of my inchoate literary potential."

She slugged back a good splosh of Merlot.

"I want a signed copy of the first book. Tell me more about Betty

Black."

Statement to police, cont'd...

At closing time, we left the pub. We stood on the pavement regarding each other in the cliché timeframe of the pre-snog moment. We snogged with a degree of tenderness.

"Call my number then we'll be connected," she demanded as she lit up a Marlboro.

Really, really truly, I didn't want to do it. She'd already told me she knew where I lived.

"Well, dial the number I gave you, you fuck-wit."

I called the number and somewhere in one of her inner fleshy crevices, a device played the murder scene from Pagliacci.

"*La commedia e finita*" I said.

"You don't impress me. So, you've watched a dumbed-down opera show on BBC 4. But you're better than a load of other *drongs* I've wasted time on."

"I imagine you had a university education?"

"Well you imagine pretty good. Imagine me as a first at Oxford and a master's at Cambridge."

"You'd think the women would be mistresses wouldn't you?"

"If I were you, I'd stick to shit driving. You've got a bit of superficial low-class wit but that's just an ironic self-mockery at your life failure. You might impress some tart in a chip shop but don't try it on with me."

"I rather fancy a bag of chips. I'll leave you to go back to your intellectual castle. Good night," I said.

"Don't you just walk away from me after you've debased me. How fucking dare you? How fucking dare you?"

"Betty, I'm a free man. I don't want to be rude or unpleasant."

"Man? What sort of fucking man are you? I've selected you. I'll give everything of myself to you. I'm so sorry Oscar. I was horrible wasn't I?"

"A harsh man might say so."

A looping fist slammed into my nose. The hot tip of her cigarette burned my cheek.

"You moron. You revolt me," she added.

"Was that a mood swing?" I asked, stepping back out of range.

"Left hook."

"Betty, this isn't for me, OK. I respect you as a poet but that's it."

"Poet? You think I'm a fucking poet? Fucking sonnets give me Shelley belly. I just stab down any old word and you *drongs* think it's clever. I hate poetry. I loathe myself as a pseud arty-farty feather in the fucking wind. Poetry is useless boring shit but no one wants to admit it. Fuck off."

I turned and walked away. I could hear her sobbing. I made it to Mick's Fish Bar in the High Street and ordered battered jumbo sausage, pea fritter and chips. The pea fritter was extravagant but I kind of felt like a condemned man. My phone was ringing. I just knew...

"You've made a big mistake leaving me like that. You started something, Mister and you think you can just turn your back? Think again loser."

I clicked off and took my meal.

"*La commedia non e mai finita*," I said to the woman behind the counter.

"I'd love a man who could woo me in Italian," she replied.

Well, Betty was right. I could make an impression in a chip shop.

I decided to dine al fresco. Something told me that Betty might not be going straight home and she knew where I lived. I sat down on a wall at the back of the Southleigh night club and munched to a serenade of boom-boom bass. A rat ran along the brickwork and took a flying leap at my sausage. The back entrance of the club opened and a client was hurled out into the night by a mob of bouncers. He kicked at the door as it slammed. I chose not to empathise with the guy about the harsh injustice of life and the struggle for existence, as symbolised by the rat. For sure I could work it into a poem for the next meeting. Maybe I'd had enough of that useless boring shit. Did I want to be a pseud arty-farty feather in the wind? I made my way back to Mutton Street using the back alleys. I climbed the back fence and entered the house from the rear garden. I kept the lights off and peered out past the old blanket which formed my curtain. Sure enough she was outside, leaning on the high brick wall of the cable works opposite my window. She was on her mobile. My phone was ringing. I clicked it off, but she must have just caught the sound. Her heels tapped across the tarmac. I withdrew into the darkness of my room. She was in the front garden and had her face right against the single glazed window.

"You cringing excuse for a man. Coward—come out and face up to what you've done."

I just didn't want this kind of trouble. Her dark smoky voice was muttering threats and oaths. She began to tap the glass and then slap harder. I was about to confront her when the window of the bedroom above me opened and the Polish guy Kaz shouted.

"You, you piss off you bitch, or I smack your face."

"Don't tell me to piss off in my own country you Slavic cabbage-boiler."

"I come now to smack your face."

Betty picked up the underlying toughness in his voice and retreated.

"Hey Polski—just know that the worm hiding in that front room is a liar and a rapist. If you want a face to smack you could do a public service."

"Oscar is not rapist. He is pathetic old shit-man,"

"Ask him."

"He'll say no."

"I told you he's a liar."

"You go to the police if he raped you. If you want, you can go with a smack in the face, you understand? I come now."

Betty raised her two fingers at Kaz.

"Up yours Polski twat."

By now she had retreated to the other side of the street and began to walk away. I watched her get to the corner and slumped down on my bed and started to get into my sleeping bag. My phone sounded its message tone.

"*Nessun*-fucking-*dorma* you pseudo opera expert. I've got the words and music to all your numbers. I'll put the *Turandots* on your eyes. I shit on your fake cultural references. I trump your pathetic house of auto-didactic cards. Sweet dreams xxxxx."

There is a lot to be said for a university education.

The police lady took another swig of wine to finish her drink and flexed her writing hand.

"I've got another bottle somewhere."

"That's OK. Did you think of calling the police?"
"And tell them that an attractive educated woman wanted me?"
"Well, no one would believe that. Maybe just that a woman was breaching the peace?"
"Well, I'm a trainee romantic novelist and an established local poet. I understand passion and the dark stirrings of the inner soul."
"Did you think that was the end of it?"
"I knew it wouldn't be."
"So, what happened then?"

Statement to police cont'd...

I got some sleep and went to work in the morning. My phone rang and text messages poured in all day. Some were hostile threats, some were declarations of love, some were tortured self-loathing at her debasement before me, some were accounts of her dampened underwear. There were a few close-up shots of bodily things she had that I might like. I have the pictures on my phone, but I don't want to embarrass her. I would never expose a lady to ridicule or unfavourable gynaecological comparisons.

I had a full day of foul-sewer pumping. There are some exclusive organic watercress beds in the north of the county and the local domestic excrement levels could flood into them. I worked my tanker between a cathedral of vegan health and the nearest sewage farm. About midday, the office phoned me and told me a woman kept calling to tell them I was a rapist and that she wanted some manure on her strawberries. The boss told me they could not be smeared with that kind of rape-shit and they might have to fire me to show political correctness. Then the personnel woman called me to say they wanted me for an interview.

"Do you think I'm a rapist?" I said.
"Can't see how you'd get consensual intercourse," she replied.
"Why can't you just say sex?"
"You see—you're obsessed. I'm trained to spot trigger warnings and subliminal deviancy. I've also been trained to report suspicious Muslims. I've noted your response on your file. Be here for formal interview Monday morning at 11 o'clock."
"I'll plead guilty to suspicious Muslim if you drop the rape charge?"

"Sparrow—you're in the shit. One more racist slur and it's instant dismissal."

"Look—Jean, you've known me for years."

"Nine months and four days. I've just checked to see how cheaply we can kick you out," she corrected me.

"That's a lifetime to an artist. We try to die young to claim immortality."

"We'll try and get you some hospital surgical waste jobs. Should get a dose of TB if you spot a bit of lung."

"Thanks, Jean."

"You're welcome, Sparrow."

She's an OK woman but she has a job to do. The customers don't want rapists with thick hoses applying suction to their domestic pipes.

So, I finished my shift and drove home. I kept my lights off and didn't answer my phone. Several times I heard her talons clacking on the pavement outside. About nine o'clock, Kaz shouted out the window at her and told her to fuck off. I tried to sleep and spent my time thinking about where my life was going. Just today I'd heard a lady on the radio and made my first ever firm life-plan. My quest is to become an Amazon number one best-selling author. I want that validation as a human being before I die. I'm not going to settle for a quick two minutes of Sid Vicious singing *My Way* at my funeral. I'm going to stop at nothing. Tomorrow I'm going to get to the book shop and get some self-help manuals like *How to Write Books*.

Tonight, I came home to begin my new life and a brick came through the window. I have to see it all as an omen pointing my way to an understanding of the heat and passion within a woman. Then I met you and you were destined to be the first to share my story. I've just got to package and bottle this torment and the world of literature will be mine.

Statement to police concluded.

The beautiful police lady let out a long sigh.

"I hope you make it, Oscar. In the meantime, what would you like the police to do with Betty Black?"

"I don't really want her to be in trouble. She's a corporate lawyer with degrees from Oxford and Cambridge. That's a lot of back and forth travel with all those heavy books. I can see how a woman like that could lose her senses over a man like me."

She ignored my witty self-deprecation.

"The windows belong to your landlord I assume?"

"I'm sure she'd pay."

"I know Mr. Singh, he's a keen businessman. If he gets compensation, he won't want to waste time in court."

"I've never met Mr. Singh. He sends a big guy in a turban for the rent. He likes cash."

"We'll keep your statement on file. In my experience you've got an ongoing issue here, Mr. Sparrow. I'll be amazed if we don't meet again."

"That would be so lovely. I've not dared to read your name badge because it's pinned to your body. The male gaze can offend."

"PC Judy Jones."

"Don't you do women police officers anymore?"

"No—I never was one. I'm too young to have ever been officially fixed as a woman."

"Tell the boss, you're doing a great job just the same. You have the genuine look, the feminine beauty, the voice and everything."

"Thanks for the drink. It's been great to meet you. My guess is that she'll be cautioned for breaching the peace and warned not to come back here. My professional assessment is that she's barking, clever and fucking dangerous. Keep safe Oscar—the world needs poetry."

"Don't forget the passionate romance. That's where I'm headed. That poetry stuff is for haggis, skylarks and lonely wandering with Ozymandius"

She picked up her pile of papers and left. I sank back into the slightly perfumed vacuum of her courageous absence and flicked shards of glass from my Pot Noodle. It was a Friday night. And, a virgin world lay spread before me, begging for a dark broad-shouldered conqueror.

4 CHAPTER FOUR

Weekends I drive a taxi. European regulations on drivers' hours do not allow such criminality, so I'm in your hands comrades. Southleigh has the one taxi company called *Alpha Cars*. The company name arose from the proprietor who had been a body builder and postman called Ron, who used to pose with baby-oiled muscles for *Men's Musk* magazine. The editor had once made him the cover model wearing his postie hat under the banner *Alpha Mail*. He had never lived it down.

    A few months ago, an Uber operator was spotted in the High Street. His burned-out car is still on the waste ground next to the old Co-op supermarket. An effigy of an Uber driver hangs from the 'Welcome to Southleigh' sign as you enter the borough. The globalized gig economy has launched attacks on our citadel but so far, we're standing firm. I've got a tracker and cab camera in my truck so the bosses can monitor my nose picking and any flatulence. I'm on a final warning for scrotum scratching at the wheel. The regime at *Alpha Cars* is far more relaxed and I need the money. Previous meanders down the gentle valley of love have left me indebted and dispossessed. I own a yellowing plastic 1970's alarm clock radio with red display numbers, an electric kettle, a nylon sleeping bag and a 1995 Mark One Ford Mondeo, which just at present doesn't have a test certificate. I have a library of romantic fiction and a soup spoon. I used to keep a can-opener but I heard a radio show about mindfulness and reduced my complexity. I'm a passive minimalist.

My plan was to pick up the cab at about midday and work through until the pubs and clubs chucked out. Normally I expected to finish at about 4am on the Sunday morning and go home with a kebab, a Sunday Mirror newspaper and half a bottle of vodka to settle myself psychologically for the working week ahead. Suddenly a new vista had opened before me. So many self-help books lay abandoned in the ruins of my bin-bagged history. Why did my women want to keep them? There was only one message:

Never ever *ever* give up on buying self-help books. Even in your last moments there will be a little high-lighted golden coin of a phrase to get you over the river Styx.

I dressed and prepared myself to walk into town to buy a book on writing books. As I reached the front door, Mr. Singh's enforcer pushed me back down the hall.
"You're out my friend. You've lost your month's deposit and we want another five hundred cash for the windows."
"I see what you're saying, sir. Just at this moment I can't put my hands on cash."
"I'll walk you to the bank."
"I'll be OK, I look too poor to get mugged."
My thought was to escape with my car keys and never be seen again. The sale of my abandoned possessions could probably raise Mr. Singh at least twenty pounds. The enforcer read my mind.
"Give us your keys now."
"No."
His huge hand gripped my face and pushed me against the wall.
"Maybe a stroll wouldn't be so bad," I said.
We made our way to the Santander ATM in Market Street. I punched in my pin.
"I can only get three hundred."
"You can get more at the counter."
"I gather you've done this before."
My account balance flashed up on the screen. £511.08p.
"Your luck's in my friend."
He gripped my arm and shoved me towards the cashier's window. He maintained his grip while I addressed the achingly pretty young girl.

"My accountant here is concerned there might be a banking liquidity crisis. His advice is to withdraw all my funds before the rush sets in."

"We ain't heard nothing," said the coltish love-nymph.

"The government is keeping the lid on over the weekend. It's nothing personal or against Santander. I love the Spanish."

"We can give you five hundred and ten pounds and eight pence. You need to leave one pound to keep the account open."

I glanced at the enforcer.

"Is that sound impartial financial advice?"

"Yeah."

His grip was hurting my arm. The girl handed me the money. Her eyes darted between my face and that of my turbaned accountant.

"Thank you. Have a nice day," she said.

We exited the bank like kids in a three-legged race. With his free hand he snatched the money and handed me a tenner. The eight pence spilled to the ground. I grovelled around to retrieve it.

"Look after the detail and the big picture will look after you," I said. "That's the first line in J.D. Goldmeyer's book *The Seven Days of Wealth Creation for Evolutionists*."

"I ain't read it my friend. Let's get back and you're off. Don't think of coming back."

To be frank I'd made a decision not to oppose his plans for me. He outweighed me by about five stones, had maybe a foot in height and twenty-five fewer years of struggle on this planet. Although he had my five hundred pounds, I had intact bones and was breathing without pain. Every bold text of every positive thinking handbook was scrolling before my eyes. We passed a homeless guy in a doorway. His dog on a hairy string whimpered at me. I threw him the eight pence.

"Fuckin 'hell, Mr. Big—go steady," said the beggar sneering at the pennies.

Just for a second an anger rose in my chest. Then the bold text of Dale Carnegie's masterpiece *How to Win Friends and Influence People* flashed before me:

Point Five: 'Show respect for other people's opinions and see things from their perspective.'

I walked on in calmness and understanding towards a new chapter in my life. The enforcer provided a free bin bag and within a few minutes I was loading it into the back of my car which was parked down the street. Life was good. I had ten pounds and time to get a book on writing. I thought of registering at the library, but the self-help books are always out and you need an address. OK, I was homeless and destitute. I was facing investigation by the sewage company for rape. I was already on final warning for genital adjustment whilst in motion at the Queen's highway in a heavy goods vehicle. How long would it take me to create my own Ricardo di Napoli and for the big bucks to come rolling in? Oh, sweet woman of BBC Radio 4—wait for me—I'm on my way.

A taxi driver can get to read quite a few books. My next self-help purchase would be the most critical choice of my life. I walked to W.H. Smiths. The pale young guy behind the counter nodded in recognition.

"How did you get on with *Millionaire in Your Mind, Billionaire in your Balls*?" he asked.

"Still on it in my lorry cab. Looks like once I've read the book, I've got to buy some pricey tablets and go on a residential course."

"Yeah, some self-help runs that kind of marketing strategy."

"Hey—you can help me with self-help. I'm training to be a writer."

"Self-help, that's cool. We've got three books on how to write self-help best sellers for beginners."

"I'll try that once I'm a big author. I'm going to write for Frills and Spoons. There's one of their top people waiting for my submission."

"Wow—they burn a lot of pulp writers. Three weeks on the shelf and that's it. They stay on Amazon digital forever like microwave echoes of the Big Bang."

"That's a great image."

"I read it in *Digital Marketing for Astrophysicists*. That's my degree. I've self-published a few books."

I stared at him. This weedy guy was light-years ahead of me. He was already an author. I was not about to accept a third humbling of the day.

"I'm the winner of the Southleigh Poetry prize. I'm the Poet

Lorry-Park."

"Poetry—that's boring shit. No one likes it but no one wants to admit it. I sold a Seamus Heaney last year. The manager put a silver star on my file for that."

"Why is a literary astrophysicist working in here?"

"Learning the craft. Working on my characterisation, developing my unique story arc style. Building a digital platform and learning my own authentic voice as an artist. I'm doing an online course with Brown Nose Creations. They're a top agency and they can get you a deal if you do all their courses. I guess I'm just waiting for that breakthrough like everyone else."

"Everyone else?"

"Yeah—most people have self-published a book on Amazon. It's like something for your Linked In profile."

"I haven't got a book out."

"Well, you know—you're kind of senior. If you know some big shot in romance, you'll be fine."

"I don't know her personally yet."

"Ah—might be a problem. Don't tell me you fell for that *seeking talented new voices* pitch?"

I nodded glumly.

"Well, we've all been there. Mugs get excited and buy a whole load of books to work out the style. My advice is to join the *League of Love Writers' Guild.* They network and give each other prizes. That way you get lit-cred and creep up the ladder."

"Do they accept trainees and sewage drivers?"

"I'm not a member. I wouldn't stress the *sewage* but they kind of loiter around in the lingerie ambiance. I can't identify with the broad-shouldered handsome hunk. Guys like us have to work with what we know."

"I'm going to work with what I dream."

"Surrealism—that's boring shit like poetry but no one wants to admit it."

"Did you go to Oxford, Cambridge or both?"

"Got a masters at the South Coast University. Astrophysics and Digital Marketing is a great combo. I'd never have got a job in W.H. Smiths without it."

"What sort of book really sells?"

"Celebrity chefs writing about their pets."

"How about a sewage guy's reverse cook-book? You know working back from my end, anus, rectum, small intestine, duodenum, up through the swallow reflex and a big spill out into the groves of Tuscany."

"You need to get famous first. There's an afternoon cable TV talent show for *wrinklies*, if you can't stomach serial killing."

I felt crushed as I sloped off to the self-help section. I needed at least one pound for some food, so I had to spend wisely. Once I took over the taxi, I could get some cash together. I scanned the shelves and there was just the one book that seemed to say it all. The title called to me: *The Gold In Your Gutter*. The tag line read, *The best seller for authors that's gonna change your life.*

I looked at the price—£9.99. This was a best seller that was already changing my life. It would mean no lunch and destitution. These were the hard times a writer needed. The sewage company was going to help me catch TB, if they didn't fire me. If I could get on Amazon Digital, I'd achieve immortality with the other millions.

I paid for the book and turned the corner. I had an important mission. I was going to use everything I'd learned from Donald Trump's book, *The Art of the Deal*. The homeless guy was still there. His greasy woolly hat was half full of change. I tossed him my last penny coin.

"I made up your final salary. You're fired," I said.

The dog on the hairy string growled. I believe he sensed my new aggression. I was already a man with gold in his gutter.

5 CHAPTER FIVE

I marched into the *Alpha Cars* office. Venus, the heavenly rounded but smouldering controller shot me an arrow of hostility.

"Some bloody woman keeps phoning for you. Won't say who she is but wants you to drive her."

"Drive her where?"

"Won't say. I told her to fuck off and she told me I had herpes."

"Sounds like an educated corporate lawyer-type."

"I told her to pop round and I'd help her with her manners."

Surely I was free of her? A few hours in the cells would surely have calmed her. I needed to pull a stunt with Venus.

"I need a favour...,"

"You've got no money and you need to take the car on credit and pay us when you've done few jobs? You've been evicted so you're desperate and homeless?"

"How did you know?"

"I met Spike the Bike at the burger van on the industrial estate. He saw your perp walk with the bin bag. He asks if you want anybody murdered. Is he your gay lover?"

"I don't want just anyone murdered. He could start with someone with degrees from Oxford and Cambridge. So, Venus—can you help me?"

"Fuck off, Oscar. No cash no car. You know the boss."

"He looked great in baby oil but generally I don't like to remind people."

I allowed an edge of *Trumpian* menace into my voice.

"He was a gorgeous guy once; runner up in *Mr. Southern Abs 1971*."

"Help us out, Venus—please?"

"Just this once, Oscar. I've left a bit of fuel in her to get you going."

"I love you, Venus. If you weren't with the boss, I'd whisk you away to paradise—just you and me."

"I could get a quickie divorce. Where shall we go?"

"Pontins at Bognor."

"I'll let you know. Soon as you've got the rent, get back in here."

At last, an act of kindness. The system was that the drivers rented the car and paid for the fuel. *Alpha Male* charged £120 for the rental. A decent guy would triple his money if he didn't have too many non-paying runners. At the thin end of the month you could budget on two or three in a shift. Venus had cut me that little sliver of luck that all creative artists need. Now I could begin to re-build my life. This was Vincent's tube of mortgaged yellow oil paint that gave *Sunflowers* to the world.

"I genuinely truly love you, Venus. May I kiss all or any of your lips?"

"Piss off and get the rent. Don't tell anyone I've gone soft."

I slid into the driving seat of a twelve-year-old Nissan. The springs and cushion had been replaced by a square of chipboard. There was an aroma of vomit and chilli sauce. The warmth of my heart flowed out to Venus. How well I could show her the heat of a man's love if she yearned for my touch. She deserved such a reward. I joined the queue of cabs on the bus station rank. A few short-run shoppers and a guy celebrating an early win at the bookies netted me enough cash to half-fill the fuel tank. My life was starting to rebuild. Another hour got me a squashed Mars bar and a half-price pork pie from the ASDA bargain bin. Sometimes a man gets a bit of luck. On impulse I swung into the railway station and picked up a guy who'd missed his stop—what cabbies call a railway sleeper. The fare was £40 and he bunged me a tenner. It gave me enough to pay the car rent and it was only seven o'clock. The night was young and long. I rejoined the taxi rank and started to read a chapter of my book entitled *How to pump out pulp like the pros*. This was the sort of inside track I wanted. I felt sure there'd be a section on how to pump out Mann-Booker and Nobel prize stuff further into the book.

My mobile phone was ringing. It was Venus.

"Oscar—looks like there's a good job at the Holiday Inn. I'm still thinking about your offer of Bognor. The guy on the desk has asked for you for some reason. Looks like there's a bit of luggage to shift. The punter wants the cab for a couple of hours."

"I love you Venus—right from that first moment our eyes made love, dancing in a melody of passion."

"You hadn't better be on the weed in one of our cabs. Have you got the rent yet?"

"Yeah."

"How long could we have together at Bognor?"

I hung up with a big kiss on the mic'. She was a lovely thing that Venus.

Greed is the provisional wing of ambition. I learned that in *Money Changing for Christians.* In anticipation, I started the meter and breezed into the Holiday Inn, ready to offer an obsequious masterclass in servile tip-grovelling. I knew the desk guy.

"Second floor 205, Oscar—lady says she needs a full personal service and we've got no porter."

"Thanks for asking for me."

"I didn't. She said you were her regular."

I shrugged. You do get punters who like a particular driver. Pound sterling signs filled my comic strip eye sockets. Minute by minute I was climbing back to an holistic dignity. I knew I needed more dietary fibre but for now I was concentrating on my emotional development.

I knocked the door. It flew open. The gorgeous naked woman in front of me spread her legs and ran her hand down over her fur-like pubis. I tried not to stare. It was definitely one I'd already seen on my phone. With her other hand she grabbed the neck of my T-shirt and tried to drag me into the room.

"You sweaty wrinkled little low-life. I despise myself for this more than I despise you," growled Betty Black.

"Be gentle with yourself, go placidly amid the noise and haste. Learn to forgive." I replied as my flimsy green Heineken pub quiz souvenir ripped down to my navel.

"We can be together. We can multi-compose the poetry of love you fuck-wit. Can't you see the shame I'm going through to offer myself like this?"

"Betty—I'm not ready for commitment. I'm flattered by your uncontrollable passion, but I can't offer you the life you deserve."

"You think I'm out of control, you patronising gargoyle. All of my brakes are on boy. Just watch out if I let rip."

Just then the fabric of my T shirt gave way and she crashed backwards into the room. I turned and fled along the corridor. Within seconds Betty leapt onto my back, gouging at my eyes with her considerable nails. The rest of my shirt fell away and I was conscious of her hot, cloying, lady-equipment pressed into the small of my spine as she wrapped her legs around my waist. I felt a stab of concern for my situation. I was topless except for my official municipal taxi badge with a naked woman on my back.

"Betty, I'm going down the steps and if you don't let go, you're coming with me."

"Don't *Betty this* and *Betty that* with me! You're not my equal."

I struggled my way down the stairs. I could feel a trickle of blood from my eyelid. I arrived at the ground floor where a vestibule opened out into the restaurant area. Several diners were at tables.

"I think there's a cabaret darling." said a lady to her sedate gentleman partner.

Betty appeared to hear the remark and sprung from my back. She planted herself hands on hips in front of the woman.

"Cabaret, you stupid old bitch? Cabaret? This is emotional drama. This is pure ugly physical desire. This is fucking love!" she bawled.

I saw the desk guy and a security guard charging towards us. I must admit I just panicked and ran out to my taxi. I floored the pedal and put distance between myself and the hotel. My eye was swelling and there were scratches down my cheeks. I needed to clean up and get a shirt. The taxi radio crackled. It was the masterful *Alpha* boss.

"Sparrow—what the fuck? What the fucking fuck, you cunt."

"I think you've put things rather well," I replied.

"Get back to the Holiday Inn. You've left your bloody wife there."

"I'm not married."

"Whatever she is. She's told the desk guy you abandoned her as a child-bride after you obtained her from a paedophile dating service on the dark web. She's spent her life searching for you."

"She's a mad woman. I haven't even got a normally illuminated web."

"Just go back and get her."

"No."

"Then bring the car in and finish up. I always thought you were a waste of space. Now you've lost us the Holiday Inn account. I'll make sure you live to regret that."

"Cheers, boss."

I drove in and walked to the office. Alpha Male was pacing the floor. The whiteness of his face flashed the danger indicator of serious repressed anger as I'd read in *Teach Yourself Body Language*.

The counter was between him and me. I knew to remain out of his fighting arc from my *Martial Arts for Cowards Manual*.

"When word hits the streets you're a *pedo*, you're dead meat in this town, you prick."

"You know I'm not a *pedo*."

"That woman says you're a *pedo* and you've lost me a top account. Fuck off."

"Think nice thoughts," I offered.

Deeper in the office I could see Venus. Her face was red and she was crying. My heart went to her, although I kept my body out of attack range. I put the rent money down on the counter.

"I've dealt with the stupid cow for breaking my rules. Just get out before I put myself in line for a five-stretch."

I let out a sigh and held out my hands in a gesture of conciliation.

"If it helps, I'm sorry," I began.

His fist whistled past my face as I turned and bolted out into the yard. Once I hit the street I looked back. *Alpha Male* had come out to the cab and threw my new writing bible in an oil drum filled with old food wrappings, alimentary canal contents and taxi-life detritus. Once he returned to his headquarters I snuck back and retrieved it. It was a small victory in what had otherwise been a negative experience.

It was cold without a shirt. My only refuge now was my faithful Henry, the 1995 Mark 1 Ford Mondeo. I had eighteen pounds forty-three pence and an empty bank account. I walked to Mutton Street. The first thing I saw was Spike, the Hell's Angel guy standing by my car in his stiff urine-treated originals and leathers. He spoke in a surprisingly light but psychopathic voice.

"You've got to kill her man. She's a crazy cock-sucking, pussy bucking, frantic hot sex-bitch."

"How do you know?"

"She told me. I slammed her one in the kisser when I saw her wrecking your ride. I'm a man who stands tall for a friend Oscar but why don't you just sort her out—I mean I would."

I looked at my car. The glass was all gone, the door mirrors lay like sparkly crumbs on the tarmac. Every panel was dented and scrawled with words like *Pedo*, *Rapist, Loser*. It looked like she had used the edge of a brick and a black spray paint.

"Only one of those words is true," I said.

"It's obvious you're a *dope*." said Spike.

"It doesn't say that. It says *Pedo*."

"Are you mocking my dyslexia?"

Spike looked angry. He was a sound guy in a scary way and I didn't have too many friends.

"Sorry mate, I was trying to be cheerful. She's right about the *loser*."

"That's OK. She needs killing or hot sex action—just say the word." Spike performed a pantomime of throat cutting and pelvic thrusting in case I hadn't understood.

"Women are dangerous to a man," he said.

"They're even more dangerous to other women."

"Everyone knows that. That's why I've never gone lesbian. Take my number in case you get desperate." said Spike.

We exchanged phone numbers and embraced like monochrome movie partisans before the final shoot out at the mountain hideaway.

The driver's door was too deformed to open so I climbed in through the window. I pushed in the key and she fired up. I needed to get somewhere where Betty Black would not and could not be. I had enough for a *Bombay Burster* from *Nazir's Furnace* takeaway and a half bottle of vodka. I had my sleeping bag and my writer's bible. Tomorrow was Sunday and I could tour the newsagents' windows seeking out rooms to rent. I'd been through my trial in the way that Don Trump had learned the art of dealing. I felt him at my side and engaged gear. Watch out world, I'm coming for you. It's going a be a special thing. A very special thing. A beautiful thing.

6 CHAPTER SIX

There's something refreshing about a night drive in an open car. Some people choose exotic cabriolets, but a glassless Ford Mondeo can achieve the same sense of abandon and liberation at a fraction of the cost. It was a fresh autumn evening as I pulled up at Nazir's international fast food caravan on the Southleigh industrial estate. I ordered a *Bombay Burster*—filled nan bread, with chips. I stood in the urine-scented ambiance next to the overflowing waste bin. A group of hot-hatch boys clustered around a Vauxhall Astra with two inches of ground clearance, threw hostile glances at my wheels.

"Looks like someone caught up with a *pedo*," growled one hideous home-tattooed weakling.

"I'm standing up for due process of law. It's a mobile exhibition to remind society of its fundamental values," I replied.

"What?"

"Innocent until proven guilty, due process of law."

"Yeah like some perv, kiddy-fiddling innocent little ones."

The group sensed my urbane sophistication and desire for civilised discourse and started to close in. Nazir thrust my feast at me. His black beard towered above me from the caravan like a dark vulture of testosterone-soaked doom.

"Fuck off, Oscar and don't come back."

I felt a stab of righteous outrage.

"I'm not a *pedo*."

"Someone thinks you are, and someone's scratched your face, that's all I'm saying."

I snarled at the lynch mob, strolled to my car like a blameless man and hit the gas. Jeers and laughter followed me until I was out of sight. I just had to get the vodka and I could live to fight on. Something had gone wrong with our society's perception of justice.

I felt free. Free of possessions, free of any attachment to the human race. A lunatic woman had sprayed *Pedo* on my car and I was doomed to suffer righteous mob violence. The glittering prizes were for the dentally perfect, wearers of salmon-pink trousers in Waitrose, university types and social media vegan gurus. I sucked shit and I had nothing except a bottle of vodka, a six-pack of Irn Bru and a luke-warm nan bread curry. I headed for the Abbeystoke fishing lakes, where an anti-social drunken loner could pass for a respected nocturnal sportsman and vice versa. I drove into a copse and took to my sleeping bag. By midnight I was bloated, incoherent and in oblivion.

By 4am I was in the cells. I could recall the wet drag of rotting leaves against my cheek and a raising up of my body into a van. I also remember asking someone if they were by any chance *the Gream-Ripper*? There was a face at the little flap in the door of my shit-scented concrete vomit chamber. I knew I was drunk and in trouble but before me was a vision of salvation. A woman. A beautiful woman who had already shared my bed and my Aldi Merlot.
"You're shivering," she said.
"Yes, could I have a blanket do you think?"
"Nah—you might self-harm by hanging."
"No chance, I've out-sourced self-harm and just accept the corporate dividends."
"I'm not sure if you don't care, Oscar, or if your caring circuits are disconnected as a coping mechanism."
"I might flash up with a jump start, if you've got some leads?"
"Oscar, I'm a professionally caring person. I heard you'd been arrested for drunk in charge of a motor vehicle?"
"It's my home."
"And an offence against Section Five, Road Traffic Act 1988."
"That was a top year for Merlot," I quipped, suddenly realising that I was in deep, deep shit. This could be the end. They could take

my Class One Heavy Goods driving license and everything would be over. I needed a lawyer and to think.

"How did I get here? I wasn't harming anyone."

"A patrol got a call to a sex-offender in the fishing lake woods. You were drunk in the back seat. What the hell happened to your car?"

"It's a custom job. I'm thinking of marketing them as the Ford Outcast."

"I need you to be serious for once. It was that bloody Betty wasn't it?"

"I do have reason to believe that, Constable."

"Do you want her brought in?"

"I don't want anyone brought in, locked up, reviled, punished or despised. She's a woman confronted with an irresistible temptation."

Constable Jones's face blossomed into a sunburst smile framed in the flap of the cell door."

"That's you I guess?"

"It's me as poet and artist, not merely this misshapen criminal beneath your gaze."

I heard the sound of keys and locks. I stood up to greet a true lady as she entered. She motioned me to sit down on the concrete ledge that served as bed and designer interior.

"Here's the good news. There was no sign of a car key in your property so there was no chance of you driving the car whilst drunk."

"Sure, I've got a key," I protested.

"If I say there wasn't a key there *wasn't* a fucking key."

Suddenly I saw the feral bearer and suckler of cubs, that lurks in the shadows behind even the most angelic of females. I caught her meaning and grabbed the rescue rope.

"I pushed the car there—it's got no engine."

"Fine. It's also got no road tax and no test certificate. Under sections 173 to 175 of the Transport Act 2000, police have the power to seize and destroy it. In short it's been taken to the crusher."

"Not Henry—anything but that, please?" I said, quickly realizing that had she decided to throw books at me, I could have opened a shop on eBay. Another thought crowded in. "My bin bag—my library of romantic fiction and literary self-help bible? My sleeping bag, my soup spoon and my dated red digital display clock radio?"

"It's all here. Sober up and you're out of jail."

"Thanks," I said. "I'm on the bottom and fighting to stay cheerful. I wouldn't admit that to anyone but you, Judy. They say a man and a woman can't be friends and I can see that with a beautiful lady like you, there would be temptation. All the same I could overlook any lapses into heterosexual intimacy and still take you to the pub for football arguments and fart openly in your presence."

She laughed. A beautiful laugh.

"I can't say I don't like you. There's a six-feet-four hunk of a riot cop in bed between you and me."

"Would he like to be a triangular torso in my first romantic novel?"

"He's already in mine. Oscar—it's not my place to say but you've got to wise up and get a grip of your life. You're a victim."

"They have those on BBC Radio 4 and you have to talk very nicely to them. None of them are unattractive late-middle-aged white males."

"You're choosing victimhood as an inverted status badge. I've done all the courses. You have to fight back, make a stand."

I admit it, originally, I'd just felt lust for her. I realized my emotions were deepening in the way that Ricardo di Napoli's heart had opened to his nubile young serving maid with her early morning delivery of hot muffins to his bedside.

"Don't worry Judy. One day soon I'm going to be a number one best-selling author on Amazon. I'm even going to have my own box set. I'm going to wait on my author platform for the express train to fame and riches, and I'm going to make you a star in my *Milf in the Filth* series."

"You know, I'd love that. I really would love that. You don't deserve to be where you are."

"I'm in a fantastic place, in the company of a beautiful woman who's just agreed to be my editorial consultant. Between us we're going to conquer the world."

"Before you do anything you're going to need somewhere to live and to get Betty Black out of your life. I hope you don't mind but I've monitored your phone. There's call after call, text after text, photo after photo."

"I provoke obsession in women. You're the first serious resistance I've encountered."

"She's crazy, Oscar. She believes a lowlife like you could *not* reject her. It's not about you. It's about your rejection of her. She's not for turning."

"Like Maggie Thatcher with a house brick handbag?"

"Like Theresa May with a family bible."

I looked at this woman and experienced a rare moment of focus. She was a fellow human, touched by some world-weary sense of compassion. It was dawn and she had worked all night with drunks, crooks and the tragedies of cosmic happen-stance. Yet still she had time to waste on a thing like me. I would make these women matter. I would show-case the tough love in their hearts to the world and reveal a beauty beyond all the froth of catwalks and Hollywood romance. I would create the bondage in blue sexy *Milf in the Filth* genre as a new way of being arrested by love. I assumed the inner being of Ricardo di Napoli, expanded my shoulders and grew six inches in height. I let my dark soulful eyes search for her inner core.

"I want you to know that secretly in an immature and unexpressed way that will only be revealed in my posthumous, best-selling autobiography, I will always love you," I said.

"You, Oscar, are an absolute fucking *scrote*. When you get out of here, where are you going to live?"

"My sewage truck has a sleeper cab. I'm going to try to sneak in. What time does this hotel want the rooms clear?"

"Get some sleep. I'll talk to the day shift and see if they can cut you a bit of slack. If they don't need the cell you can get a lie in."

"Thank you. Thank you," I said, as she banged me up.

Near one o'clock they threw me out. I collected my bin bag from the desk sergeant and slugged back a can of Irn Bru. There was a bag of loose change, a toothbrush and a ten-pound note.

"I didn't have a tenner," I said.

"PC Jones left it. She said she'd bought one of your books."

"Yeah, she sure did," I replied.

7 CHAPTER SEVEN

It was a long walk to the North Sidings Industrial Park where the sewage company was based. I stopped off at McDonald's for a *Big Tasty* meal, went large and took my time; about three hours. The folded-arm security guy started to pace around me as I watched the tension muscles flexing in his cheeks. It was late October and night was closing in. Darkness is the friend of the lonely since it hides that guilt of rejection that only the truly lonely know. All afternoon Betty had cascaded texts and phone calls into my despair. She also was alone in life. She'd been rejected. I understood her in the way that soldiers in the trenches must have understood their enemies; no one closer and no one further apart. I felt no malice for what had happened to me. Her obsession was probably the greatest compliment I had ever received. She was attractive and educated. The beautiful people of the literary world had turned their backs on me for all of my adult life and yet for all her allure, I wasn't ready for *Liebestod*, for the Wagnerian tragic final scene of *Shit-stain and Isolde*.

My phone battery died. My lorry cab was now my only source of hope and sustenance—it would serve as my lunar module on Apollo 13. I carried my bin bag through the quiet Sunday streets, stopping only to buy a Cornish pasty and a tube of toothpaste. Millions in this hungry war-torn world would have thought my life to be luxury. I carried that thought all the way to the North Sidings Industrial Estate. Private security guards patrolled that area and I felt sure that a rough unshaven guy alone with a bin bag would draw their attention. I kept in the shadows and ducked out of sight at the sound of a vehicle. At the end of Ballast Avenue was the yard of Interglobe Effluents with its illuminated sign reading '*Nothing Succeeds like Suck-Cess*'. I knew there were CCTV cameras on the main gates, so I dived off into a path that led to some waste ground overgrown with stinging nettles. I performed a Hollywood hero commando crawl to the back fence and looked for a weakness in the enemy lines. Eventually I found a spot where I could lift the chain link and slither underneath. In a few paces I reached my truck, recovered a spare key from the battery cover and jumped up into the cab. I saw the headlamps of a security van. I must have triggered a low level infrared beam. If they didn't spot me, they'd write it off as a fox or cat. I locked the door and scrambled up into the bunk behind the driver's seat. There were several guards and a snarling dog outside. A hand tried my door. The voices moved away but the alarm had been raised and I couldn't relax. In the gloom I began to read *The Gold In Your Gutter*. There was a chapter on building my profile and networking. My eyes shot to some familiar words on the page. The advice was simple. Join the *League of Love Writers' Guild*. I read on to learn that once I was a member, I would build my reputation and hob nob with agents and editors who could swiftly recognize my genius. From now on it was only a matter of time. Tomorrow was another day with problems of its own. I recharged my phone and switched on. At once texts and calls smashed like waves onto the cruel rocks of my silence. I turned it off and passed into profound sleep.

I'd survived the night undiscovered. My shift was due to start at 7am. I wandered to the office where the foreman was putting job sheets on clip boards.

"You're in for a discipline hearing at 11 o'clock, Sparrow. I've just given you a suck out at the Parkway Rail Station. Where's your company overalls?"

"Stolen off the washing line. I thought I could operate as a guerilla shit sucker."

"You're a total useless cunt," he commented.

All the same he tossed me a new bright-orange boiler suit good enough for Guantanamo Bay.

"Thanks Boss, I know you have to pay for these yourself."

"Piss off. Just be grateful there's a driver shortage. The bosses are bringing in a bus full of Romanians to replace you lot. Those blokes know how to work."

"I've heard they don't need trucks—they just suck the pipe."

"Don't forget to be here for your Human Relations interview at eleven."

I smiled. The foreman loved to taunt us with his bogey man of other-better-cheaper drivers but so far none had materialized. It was great to feel valued.

Back in my Guantanamo uniform I felt reborn. Now the engine was running I could get some warmth. I still had no money and nowhere to live but I had my pasty for breakfast and BBC Radio 4 had reunited me with the world of the higher mind which I craved. I drove to the rail station car park where I knew there would be a scrum of suited London commuters. The budget for the new Parkway had not extended to a main sewer connection so this mission was a regular. There was a procession of new 4X4 vehicles dropping off pin-striped executives and a bad-tempered scramble for parking slots. I bullied the tanker close enough to the manhole cover and started the pump. A public-school type bellowed from the driver's windows of his Porsche.

"You there, stand aside man. Get out of my way you moron, there's a country to run."

I created just a little pressure and slid the four-inch pipe into the reeking black pit. Most foul water sewage is diluted by water from baths, showers and domestic machines. This stuff was the pure uncut piss and shit. A weekend of dinner parties and rugger club fests had recently departed the richly laden bowels of the humanity clustering on the platforms. I cracked open the main valve and sent a fart of air down into the darkness. A great *bullip* of sewage stirred in the depths sending an Hiroshima of excrement and urine gas into the air. The complainants quickly closed their windows and I was left in peace. I wiped my hands and stood munching my pasty as I vented the tank and built up vacuum. I withdrew to the cab where a posh BBC presenter was interviewing the famous prize-winning novelist Noel Subjunctovitch.

"Now Noel, you've taken the innate themes of Tibetan cave painting as an atavistic foundation for this translation from the original Albanian I believe," cooed the grovelling presenter.

"Yah—it was organic—an osmosis in the sense of an evolving abstraction."

"Yes, yes—this is fundamentally the sense in which I perceived the parameters of your last novel—*The Cortex of Bile*. It was visceral in its uncompromising intellectualism."

I listened in awe. Soon this would be my world. I was distracted by a strange noise outside. I glanced down to see Betty Black in a lovely designer business trouser suit swinging her armoured briefcase at the mirror of my truck. On the fourth swipe the glass cracked. She was trying to hold her breath on account of the stench. I opened the window.

"What the fuck are you doing woman?"

She took a deep breath and started to retch. Her voice was strangled and tears poured from her eyes.

"I'm giving you seven years bad luck. You've made a mistake. You've ignored all my calls. All I've wanted to do was make things good between us. I was offering you my home in Cyprus and unlimited access to my female joys. Now you're going to pay the price."

"Betty—please."

"Fuck off. We could have been together. Why won't you let me love you?"

I studied her swollen eyes as she vomited. Mascara smeared her face. I went into a spontaneous literary stream of consciousness approach. Come on Oscar, have a heart. If this isn't love what is it? No one else had come within 200 yards of me. What is a man without compassion? I climbed down and drew near to her. She wiped slime from her mouth and drove her fist hard into my nose.

"You rotten bastard. You've ruined my life. You'd be a notifiable disease if anyone other than me would care about you."

The London train was pulling in. Politically correct, vegan, cultured university graduates elbowed each other for position at the doors. Betty staggered back and joined the throng.

"You'll regret this," she shouted.

"Have a nice day," I replied with a wave of my shitty hand.

My nose was bleeding onto my new Guantanamo outfit and now I had a smashed mirror to explain. I relaxed as I sucked out the tank and read more of my literary bible. I needed to perfect my technique of story arcs. The more I read the more I came to see that I was living in one. By the time I was loaded, there was no time to get to the sewage farm for a pump out. I dared not miss my hearing for industrial misconduct. I sloped back into the yard and informed the foreman I needed a new mirror.

"You're useless Sparrow—fucking useless and incompetent. You'll be on your way when the Romanians get here," he said.

"Don't tell me. The Romanians don't need mirrors."

"The Romanians can drive properly. They don't smash stuff up and shrug it off. They're grateful for a crust."

"I've tried reversing with crusts but you just can't see where you're going."

"That's why we all hate you Sparrow. All your sneery crap. All your Radio 4 opera and poetry bollocks. Drivers get in your truck and the radio is stuck on Beethoven and militant lesbians talking about existential clitoral identity. You're a pervert and some even say an EU Remainer."

"You're confused. I'm an oral-clitoral therapist and I'm proud of it. Poetry is boring shit but nobody wants to admit it. That's why I've renounced purity and become a commercial romantic novelist."

"There's more shit in you than there is in that tank."

"Will you be at my unbiased discipline hearing?"

"Too fucking right, I will. I'll be advising any soft cunt from the London office that we don't need airy fairy Latin gabbling twats like you."

"*Caveat Emptor. Nudus cum nudas iacebat. Nil desperandum*," I quipped.

"We all hate you Sparrow. All shit suckers despise you."

"A man is never a prophet in his own cess-pit," I countered.

I strode to my truck, my head high. Like Admiral Nelson at Trafalgar I would stand proud on the deck of my demise, certain that my victory would one day be cheered by the mob. All I needed now was a stone column of 169 feet 3 inches tall and maybe some pigeon shit to make me feel at home. Bring it on.

8 CHAPTER EIGHT

I assessed the panel of interrogators. Of course, there was the foreman, Jean the HR lady and Simon Blanchwhistle the depot manager. There were two other people whom I didn't know.

Jean was the first to speak.

"Sparrow—let me inform you that we have police Inspector Helda Bone from the Southleigh sexual offences squad and Tarquin Montacute, legal consultant to Interglobe Effluents with us today. We have taken this step because of the nature of the allegations against you. Interglobe Effluents cannot and will not be associated with any kind of perverted behaviour. Do you understand?"

"No," I retorted.

"That's because you're a stupid tricky assed prick," stated the foreman.

Tarquin Montacute took up the cudgel.

"You, Sparrow, have smeared the Interglobe Effluent brand with allegations of rape, paedophilia and licentious adjustment of your genitals whilst at the wheel of one of our vehicles. We have video evidence of your hand leaving the steering wheel whilst at a speed of 52 miles per hour and the gratuitous and vigorous fondling of your scrotum. The on-board personnel surveillance camera provides explicit footage."

"There's bugs in Mr. Singh's lodgings sir. I do often need to scratch. If something's biting your sack, surely it's safer to obtain relief when one is at high speed. I would like to say sir that in recognition of this matter I have removed myself from Mr. Singh's hospitality."

"Really—where do you live now?"

"Nowhere sir. Where can I be sure of the level of purity commensurate with employment at Interglobe Effluents?"

"You daft fucking knob-head." growled the foreman.

"May I ask a question?" I began. "I realize that the on-board personnel surveillance system can watch my every move and gesture. I will concede there may have been an incident of innocent and non-pleasurable scrotal adjustment. Do you have video evidence of paedophilia and rape?"

"It's part of a coherent and consecutive pattern of behaviour. I imagine you have never studied criminology at degree-level? I suppose you have never heard of Rolf Harris?" said Inspector Bone.

"I'm an ex-poet and developing romantic novelist. I'm useless at drawing and have never handled a boomerang." I replied.

I quickly studied my interrogator as she leafed through a thick dossier. She was a sturdy rosy-faced woman with bottle-bottom specs.

"When a shameless self-toucher or even incipient masturbator is accused of vile sexual offences, the public expects to be protected and informed. They have that right," she added.

Simon Blanchwhistle, the manager, stated the corporate attitude.

"May I add that the public cannot tolerate such a person knowing the intimate life of their internal organs or that of their innocent children."

I felt a sense of righteous exasperation.

"Look, this woman has phoned up to say I'm a rapist. She's known to police as mentally unstable."

Inspector Bone made a show of reading her notes.

"My report on her indicates signs of emotional trauma and recovered memories."

"Just take me in then. I don't know if we still have legal trials but I'm sick of this," I said.

"Exhibitions of temperament and mocking of the judicial process are not acceptable for a person representing Interglobe Effluents," said Tarquin Montacute.

"Sir, I've nowhere to live, no money, no food, no car and it looks like no job. Just lock me up and solve all my problems."

"Yes, and let the taxpayer support you," added the foreman.

Jean, the HR manager allowed a tepid smile to flicker on her lips.

"Wait outside, Sparrow. We're going to discuss your case over lunch."

"Will there be any for me? I'm hungry."

Simon Blanchwhistle closed the meeting.

"Just keep your hands out of your underpants. All Interglobe premises are under video surveillance."

I wandered over to my truck, conscious of the urge to adjust my genitals. On the pretence of checking the underside of my trailer I risked a quick hike of my underwear. No guards came running. No alarms sounded. It was small victory. I started to read *Gold in Your Gutter*. I selected a chapter on forming my own writing process. There would be a need to connect with myself, to make the writing a pleasurable activity. Inwardly I sighed. Right now, I didn't need to think of self-pleasuring. If Interglobe Effluents sacked me at least there would be an immediate payout, maybe enough to get myself another room and some food. On the other hand, few employers would want me if I had been rejected by shit-suckers. My mind flashed back to my eleven-plus exam when I'd been asked to arrange words in alphabetical order. I know I could have done it if I'd known there was an alphabet. From then on it had all been downhill with expulsions and exclusions until I could get a job as a grease monkey in a truck depot. Married at eighteen, bin-bagged at twenty-two following a moment of weakness with an irresistible launderette temptress whom no man could have resisted and apparently none ever had. Women had taken me to the pinnacle of joy. It was only because I had flown so high in adoring them that it had taken me so long to return to the ground. Right now, the cockpit emergency voice was yelling "Pull Up. Pull Up."

"Are you listening cloth-ears?"

It was the foreman at the cab door. I snapped back to the present. His face was stiff and angry.

"Yeah, what's up?"

"You'll get a final written notice about your disgusting groping at the wheel."

"Is that it? What about the rape and paedophilia?"

"They ain't got enough on you at present. That poof Montacute wasn't prepared to risk you *squinnying* to a tribunal. We've handed all the recordings of your conduct in the cab over to police. Just remember we're watching every move."

"Thanks."

"Hah, don't mention it. Once the Romanians come in all of you lot'll be out the gate. Just fuck off and get blown off at the sewage farm. Call in as soon as you're empty."

It was good to be free and on the open road. The blue lamp on the surveillance camera blinked its sly wink every few seconds. My scrotum itched but I stood tall and bore it like a man. I was hungry, not like Syrian refugees or sub-Saharan Africans are hungry—just plain rumbling and getting painful hungry. Once at the sewage plant I connected up and pumped out. I slurped my last can of Irn Bru. I needed an intervention. I needed something to change my luck. I strolled over to sit in the sun on the concrete edge of a sludge filter bed. The flow was running well through the four-inch flexi pipe. I'd run out two lengths which join together with what is known as a Bauer coupling. Without being technical, the end of one hose clips to the next hose and is shut by a lever. As I passed the fixing, my new oversized Guantanamo overall trousers snagged the lever and flipped open the joint. A plume of concentrated urine and excrement fired into the air to a height of about twelve feet. I had to regain control and dived on the leak, skilfully snapping it shut. My hair and clothing were soaked. I wiped organic substance from my mouth and eyes. Luckily there was a freshwater hose on the wall of the sludge bed. Gratefully I stripped naked in the cold air and showered myself clean. Now I really was in the shit. Nothing like this had ever happened to Francesco Romanelli or for that matter, Ricardo di Napoli.

9 CHAPTER NINE

If you're an airline pilot or ship's captain in the movies, there is always a check list and a procedure for the inevitable emergency. The handsome leader snaps out the words like "Deploy standby thrust actuators," and the side-kick replies "Check. Affirmative."

I'm thinking back to last film I watched where Tom Hanks had landed his plane in the Hudson River. He kept calm, commanding and attractive to women.

The weight of water and the worn elastic had allowed my underpants to slither to my ankles. I looked to the heavens wishing that I could break open an emergency ration of religious belief. As I stared up into the pitiless mystery of the sky, I became aware of a warm wet sensation affecting my shrivelled penis. I looked down to see the snout of an Alsatian dog nosing my groin. I followed its lead to the hand of a woman.

"Looks like you've had a Bauer coupling incident," she said.

It's rare that you can talk to a woman about sewage piping, so I tried to smile.

"You know about these couplings?" I asked.

"Fuck me yeah. When my old man was with us, God bless 'im, he had a few soakings. You're not a Romanian are you? I heard all you local boy sludge-gulpers were being kicked out."

The woman was older than me—maybe about seventy-five years old. She wore a woolly tea cosy hat, a stained duffle coat and odd Wellington boots, one black and one red. I glanced down at her dog which was growling at my genitals.

"No, I'm not Romanian. Is your dog safe around unfamiliar penises?"

"Yeah—he senses the male threat that's all. He'll be fine if you give him a good kick up the ass."

I noticed her loose-fitting false teeth and her wrinkled facial skin. Even so I could sense a girlish sense of fun and a natural feminine beauty about her.

"I'm Oscar—Oscar Sparrow the Poet Lorry-Park."

"Fuck me—you're that pervert taxi driver the fishermen overpowered in the woods when you were night prowling looking for kiddies to fiddle with."

"Bollocks—who told you that?"

"Only joking, mate. One of the anglers but he's a stupid cunt bigging himself up. I didn't believe him and that hell's angel Spike told me the real story. Spike's a friend."

"Wow—he's a good man and thanks—uh, I don't know your name."

"Roz—Roz Banks. I live up at the cottage at the sewage farm entrance. My husband worked here when it was all run by the council. That load of pirates, Interglobe Effluents, took the place over under Maggie Thatcher but part of the deal was that I kept the house until death. You look like you need a bit of help just at the moment."

Really, she was a very beautiful woman who could readily melt into my heroic arms. I felt almost felt tearful.

"You've no idea how right you are."

"I've got a couple of Denis's old council overalls and some jumpers. How do you feel about being in a dead man's underpants?"

"As long as we're not sharing."

She sniggered.

"You're a bit fucking drole, ain't ya? It will keep you going 'til you get home."

"Just at the moment I'm homeless as it happens. I might need to keep them for a few days."

I noticed her eyes appraising my body. I wanted to explain that my manhood was far more impressive in warmer weather. She appeared to nod in approval.

"Come on up to the house with me. I'll wash out your boiler suit. We might be able to sort your life out a little bit."

She concluded with a hearty wink. I looked down but nothing twitched. Maybe I was getting over women at last. She waited while I disconnected the hoses. I noticed her watching me with a kind of pleasure on her face. A lifetime of truck loading and heavy work had provided me with a reasonable physique although I was running to seed—mainly single malt barley.

"Never thought I'd watch a naked man working out in front of me again on this earth," she said.

She had a home, clothing, food and friendship. I was falling.

"Glad you like it," I said with my sexy, film-star smile.

Her dog had planted its snout between my buttock cheeks and growled again. He sensed my male threat. I collected my soaked overalls realising that my new smart phone was about as smart as a wet fag packet in the gutter.

"I'm supposed to call the office."

"You can use the house phone."

So, I did what any naked man would do and strolled along the entrance road back to her gatekeeper's cottage as if we were two regular folk on an average Monday. She gave me a cup of sweet heavenly tea, a slice of homemade fruit cake and a selection of her dead husband's clothing.

"When did Denis pass over to the other side?" I asked.

"He didn't pass over anywhere. He just croaked one night up the Albert Arms. That was about ten years ago."

"So, you've been alone for a while?"

"Yeah, on and off. Don't ask and I won't tell you, eh? I'm a woman who enjoys a bit of manly company, Oscar."

She had taken off her outdoor clothes. She was a full-bodied buxom woman and clearly still liked to hold forth her attractions. Her lush but greasy waist length hair was silver and completely straight. She was a child of the sixties in Marianne Faithful aspic. She possessed a rare loveliness that combined with the fruit cake and tea built into a symphony of feminine delight.

"You'll be looking for somewhere to stay then?" she said.

"Yes."

"Just until you can square things up, you can stay here. I'm trusting you to behave and keep eyes and your gob shut. I've got a spare room but I don't want any whores or trollops in here. The max' stay is for four weeks so you need to get on top of your life."

"I can never thank you enough."

"Don't overdo it. It's a hundred all in. Pay when you get paid. I've got some steak and kidney pie tonight."

I would have given her anything, performed any act of pleasure or kindness. She opened a tin of tobacco, rolled a cigarette and added some weed. She took a deep pull and offered it to me.

"They drug test us at Interglobe Effluents," I explained.

"Nosy pricks. A smoke does you good and I'm seventy-six. Weed's the only thing that blocks the smell of shit. When the wind is off the filter beds, it chokes you," she said.

I called in to the office. They sent me to a burst sewer near the cathedral at Hornchester. As I sucked the waste, an angelic choir was singing evensong. It was a rare moment of synthesis between heaven and the soul of a man. I was a humble creature to whom an angel had come. As the boys' voices soared into the vaulted dome of twilight, an Irish guy walked up to me.

"When you're finished could you suck out a trench for us? We're doing internet cable just over the way."

"Fifty quid cash," I said.

"Done—I'll see you round there."

An hour later I had the money and was pumping out at the Hornchester sewage works.

I had money and a place to live. Somewhere out there in the wild untamed ocean of human life, I knew Betty Black lurked like the great white in *Jaws*. Just at present, she couldn't know where I was. All the way back to the yard I kept my hands out of my underpants and sang hymns. A tide had turned and there could be no going back.

It was a two mile walk from the yard to Roz's cottage but my social agenda was clear. I must admit that I had begun to wonder how she saw the evolution of our relationship. She was seventy-six but clearly a warm and sensual person. As I approached the house, I saw a big macho-style motorcycle outside. It looked like Spike's bike. Could he have called to see me? I passed the window and saw Roz in his arms, locked in a deep kiss that had the look of wet tongues. Spike was younger than me—maybe forty-eight. I knew he didn't always come home but had never suspected any kind of love story in his life. A woman is a thing of joy and mystery to a man.

Just a glimpse of their clinch proclaimed a true emotional and erotic passion. I needed this life flow around me as I began to climb back to cruising altitude in my life; towards acceptance and the *League of Love Writers' Guild*.

I rattled the door as I walked in. Roz was pushing back her hair and re-settling her dentures. I extended my hand to shake with Spike. He smiled, shrugged and opened me a can of double strength lager.

"All turned out OK in the end mate," he said.

10 CHAPTER TEN

The living room had an old-fashioned coal fire. I dined with Roz and Spike on a sumptuous steak and kidney pie with Bisto gravy, mashed potato and a selection of vegetables. This was the full English Brexit. This was the land of Boris and Rees-Mogg. This was my return to the land of dietary fibre.

I learned that Roz often entertained Spike and had done so for a few years. It wasn't something he wished to proclaim publicly and particularly not to his chapter of bikers. It wasn't her age; it was that she was a hippy. In the flickering light of the fire I felt at last some sense of permanence and acceptance by other humans. Maybe this was happiness? I felt secure enough to reveal my inner self.

"I'm going to be a novelist," I told them.

"I hope you're not selling out to the man to pump out supermarket romance shit?" she answered.

"Shit pumping is me but I was hoping to sell out to a woman from Frills and Spoons. I'm going to write beautiful love stories."

"You going to write about that mad bitch who's wrecked your life?" asked Spike.

"Her passion and obsession, yes. Her beauty and intelligence yes."

"You're a daft twat Oscar, she's nuts. Do you want to know where she lives and get even?"

I had no idea where she lived other than it couldn't be too far away.

"Where does she live?"

"Great Western Drive, number forty-six."

"How do you know that?"

"The day you got chucked out, she came round looking for you. Kaz told her to fuck off but I followed her car."

"Why?"

"In case she caused more trouble. I wanted to know where to throw the petrol bomb."

Roz intervened, lighting up a tempting joint and already floating on the hit.

"You ain't ever going to do that Spike. I know you've got to act tough but I've got other things for you to do."

I watched in fascination as she leaned back and ran her hands tenderly over her breasts. This was not the problematic lumpen *geriatricat* that obsessed the social affairs pundits on BBC radio on account of their complex illnesses and lingering deaths in expensive social care. This was a highly sexed, pot lover who knew the vibe and clearly had an appetite for pleasure. Spike took a toke and smiled.

"Nah, I wouldn't hurt her but believe me, Oscar, she's not about to leave you in peace. I didn't hide that I was behind her on the bike. I wanted her to know that other people could take a fight to her if she wanted one."

The thought of her spoiled my contentment. Somewhere she was out there and could attack at any time. I didn't want to bring trouble to Roz's door, after all she had done for me. While it was just about me, I could see the funny side of her but I couldn't inflict her on others. Spike and Roz stood up, kissed lips softly and looked ready for bed.

"I'll do the dishes, sweet dreams," I said.

"I could get used to having you in the house," she said with a tweak of her eyebrow.

As I cleared the table, I could hear movement in the room above. It wasn't long before the sounds of female pleasure and abandon reached my ears. Finally, Spike let out a biker's bellow which I imagined was the equivalent of a perfect sustained wheelie at full throttle. I sat and watched the fire die. I disassembled my phone and left the components to dry in the hearth. Just for this moment I had peace and a home.

The next morning at the yard the foreman threw me a job sheet as I entered the office.

"Bloody phone is jammed with that fucking ex-wife of yours. How the fuck you got away with buying her as a child-bride and abandoning her I don't know."

"How can she have been a child-bride? She's about the same age as me"

"So, you were a pervert even as a kid. Just listen to the poor cow."

The foreman set the phone to speaker and played a message. The smoky rasp of Betty's voice was unmistakable.

"Please, please I appeal to the good name and reputation of Interglobe Effluents to hear my plea. One of your drivers abandoned me after he had led me on and encouraged me to debase myself. I can't offer myself to any other man now. Tell that Sparrow I can forgive him if only he will acknowledge me."

"Poor bitch—you took her honour and now you turn your back and satisfy your lusts by performing filthy masturbatory acts at the wheel."

I shook my head and walked to my truck. There was no point in denial or explanation. My job was a routine domestic suck out at some new house out of town and off main sewer. It was a place called *Silicon Palais*, with a map reference. I clipped my phone back together and amazingly it worked. As soon as I turned it on, I saw the memory was completely full of texts and the voicemail box was jammed. Within seconds it started to ring. I ignored it and found the location on Google Maps. Every time the phone stopped ringing it started again. The woman was a tireless machine. I tried to put her out of my mind by thinking of how I would write the first paragraph of my romance novel. The heroine would be a female police officer. Already I loved her, wanted to hold her. She wouldn't be like me; she would have properly elasticated underwear and be untainted by bodily behaviour.

I found the enormous house which was almost a stately home. There was an intercom on a brick pillar adjacent to two massive steel gates. Not everyone wants a thirty-eight tonne truck on a domestic drive. I buzzed and spoke in my best servile tone.

"It's the waste lorry ma'am."

"For the cess-pit?" answered a soft female voice.

"Yes ma'am. I believe you're in need of a suck."

The lady giggled.

"I'll open the gates. Follow the road right to the bottom of the grounds. There's a guy down there to show you his manhole."

Her voice was rich, sweet and bubbly like Nutella mixed with Irn-bru. I drove in past garages, a Porsche, a big Mercedes, a swimming pool, tennis courts, a sit-on mower, lawns, a lake with fish and frogs. This had to be an I.T. billionaire's place if the name of the house gave it away. Ahead of me a guy was waving and pointing to the cess-pit cover. Normally the punter quickly moves away and lets the operative do his work but he waited for me to climb down.

"Hi, there it is," he said.

He was mid-forties with quite an open innocent face, for a rich guy. He had none of the twisted selfish greed you often see in hard-nosed business graspers.

"Thanks."

"I see your tanker has a fleet serial number. Are they sequential within the business or is it a random number?"

The figures were 7532. I shrugged and shook my head. The man smiled.

"The first four prime numbers in reverse. I wonder what would be the odds of that occurring by chance?"

"I'd been thinking about that myself, sir."

"Had you? It's a quirky one isn't it. It's one of those questions that begs an algorithm."

I'd heard of algorithms because the bank had refused to extend my credit limit because of one. I'd assumed it was some kind of a phenomenon like tsunamis which occurred around Indian call centres.

"I guess you do a lot of sums, sir?" I said.

He glanced at me with a puzzled frown.

"The sum of prime numbers you mean? Yes, yes you're referring to Goldbach's conjecture?"

"Nothing else surely," I replied.

"Do you write code?"

"Only in the simplest of forms, sir. I call it poetry."

"Ah—but I bet you use Scratch to bring blocks of data together?"

"I often scratch to move my blocks apart, particularly in high humidity."

"You're an interesting man."

"You too, sir. I imagine you're into I.T?"

"Sort of – chip design and quantum concepts, but the clever money is moving into Apps."

"Like my job—Shit' Appens," I quipped.

The man spread his hands to heaven with an almost evangelical look on his face.

"What did you say? What did you say?"

"It was a weak joke, sir, you know, toilet humour?"

"A joke – toilets? I see, I think. Shit happens is a well-known expression and you said *Shit 'Appens* to configure that speech concept in the terms of an Android application?"

"Absolutely."

"So, what is the basis of your operation? How many trucks and operatives are there?"

"About a dozen. There's far more demand than trucks. Quite often it's just a blockage you can shift with drain rods."

"So—listen what if there were a platform where ordinary people with other full-time jobs, or gig workers, could get involved in sewage? Shit 'Appens could be a way of getting a drain guy just like getting a pizza delivery, or a cab?"

"They would need a suck-truck for the big jobs."

"We could offer franchises and finance, like Uber?"

"*Poober*—you could call it *Poober*, sir!"

He stared at me.

"*Poober. Poober!*" he repeated.

"*Poober*—cos shit 'appens" I said.

"You're an extraordinary man. I think this could be the new Microsoft."

"I am the Poet Lorry-Park and working on a novel."

"Keep this project to yourself. We may be able to sell it just as a concept and let someone like the Romanians develop it. The app' could show the operator how to rod a drain and lift a cover. The whole workforce could be zero-skilled and gig-waged."

"You could do a deluxe feature where the operative samples a solid specimen and offers dietary advice, or even recipes. Busy health-conscious people could just call in a guy to check out their gut. It'd be like *Just Eat* in reverse."

"*Just Shit*," he said.

"Defecation across the nation. Brilliant, sir. Pure brilliance."

I'd begun to wonder who this guy was. He seemed to be a genius very much in my own mould. I thought of revealing my invention of the reverse cookbook but figured I might be overloading him. I busied myself connecting up my hoses and opening the pit.

"Could you pop up to the house when you've finished? We'll have chat," he said.

"Sure, it's a lovely house if I might say so, sir."

"Yes, I've moved on but my ex is still here. I only popped in to see the progeny. One invests a lot of genetic optimism going forward with a breeding schedule. I heard of virtue-signalling anti-natalism too late and figured I had to do it to seem normal. Have you ever bred?"

"I'm afraid not. I've trained with live bullets, but I've always kept my head protected. I'm only fifty-seven."

"Based on average life expectancy you will die aged eighty-three. That means you are sixty-eight-point-six-seven percent of the way through your life."

"I hadn't thought of things in those terms."

"I like to base my decisions on precise figures."

"Well, you seem to have done very well, sir."

Just then there was a loud rasping sound like an extended vibrating fart. Quickly I checked all of my seals and joints.

"Don't worry—that's Michelle. Once the kids get off to school, she practises her trombone on the patio. The crows love it. It's one of the reasons we split up. Come on up for coffee when you're done."

11 CHAPTER ELEVEN

The kitchen was magnificent. It was as if a celebrity chef had joined the royal family. There was a huge central island with a black granite top. There were copper cooking pots, a coffee machine that popped in and out like a cuckoo clock, a round shouldered Smeg fridge and twelve-burner stove. I spotted a pot of Farrow and Ball Elephant's Breath paint in the hall. This was Sunday supplement on acid and not just any acid. The floor was in magnificent marble, while discreet recessed lamps provided lighting. I hesitated at the back door. Someone like me couldn't enter such a place. The gentleman of the house beckoned me in.

"I don't really like to, sir. Your home is so perfect."

"My home is in Bucharest with my partner Flavia. She can cook sew and write code all at once. You've not fully known the loveliness of a woman until you can talk digital in bed. I stick to SQL, but she's done a lot to develop my Python."

"I have been digital with women in bed, but I suppose I'm more of the analogue generation."

"I'm Nigel Simmonds, CEO of Siliconia plc."

"I'm Oscar Sparrow, the Poet Lorry-Park and romantic novelist."

"But your default position is sewage operative and now consultant to *Poober*."

"That would be an incredible honour, sir."

I decided not to enquire about payment for my services. It was heady stuff just to be considered worthwhile as a creature.

"Michelle's into all that romance. She reads about rippling Italian studs whisking stupid housewives away to Venice for nights of passion."

"Ricardo di Napoli, Francesco Romanelli," I said, wishing to expose my credentials.

A woman's voice arrived from off stage.

"Francesco Romanelli—the billionaire breeder of love children?"

My eyes swivelled to the door as she entered. Her face was wearing a smile as if it were a diamond necklace. Her lips were a perfect red like an unexpressed yet searching kiss. Her eyes were blue, clear, gentle and kind. I held her gaze, my mouth dropping open to reveal my National Health Service amalgam-filled molars. Her ample cleavage was horizontal like a central drainage channel on a French Riviera balcony. This was a woman who defined female—a lush parcel of full-bodied delight with a warm heart pumping out pure temptation like the juice of sweet late summer vines. She was a succulence and a fruitful pannier of blooms aching for harvest. I stared and stared.

"Michelle's my ex," said Nigel.

How could such a woman be an ex to any man? Even a man flattered momentarily by another woman's glance could never deny himself this overflowing oasis of passion. In my fifty-odd years at the cutting lace of the oestrogen mine, nothing like this had ever affected me in the same way. This woman was so lovely that the worn elastic of my underpants threatened to expose me as nothing other than a Pavlovian canine wretch enslaved to the male algorithm. I dared not risk a scrotal adjustment. I moved my eyes away from her lips and her Riviera balcony to look at her hands. Her fingers bore no rings, no lustrous rubies for her heart or shining sapphires for her eyes, no fire and creamy opals for her darting mystery. Had she never been worshipped? Perhaps in her yearning despair she had thrown such fecklessly offered baubles aside?

"Ex?" I stammered.

"Nigel has migrated his data onto an overseas digital platform," she said in her smooth rich voice.

I sensed an awkwardness in the discourse and offered a disingenuous distracting non sequitur.

"I've emptied your pit. You have very good cuisine as I can see from your kitchen. Your solid waste is a credit to you."

"Thank-you—you must get to see many different things," she said.

Even the idea of speaking to such a woman intimidated me. I was gabbling without thought.

"Floating turds are a sign of too much fat but here everything solid was on the bottom."

Nigel gave a small round of applause.

"That's brilliant Oscar—I'm beginning to see the potential of the *Just Shit* app. I've got to go but leave your mobile number with Michelle and I'll fix a meet with a couple of colleagues."

In a second he was gone. I stood in auto-didactic, anachronistic confusion, like a defiled Hindu untouchable before the calling flesh of Aphrodite.

The lady of the house handed me a cup of coffee from the cuckoo clock machine. All her cups, saucers and spoons matched. I had had no idea that people lived like this outside of newspaper supplements. The coffee was black and intensely flavoured. I tried not to wince. I could see the lady scenting the air. Even though I was relatively clean I worked with complex and highly aromatic compounds to which I had become immune. My earlier life had included an attempt at boxing and cruel blows to my nose had handed me the mercy of a poor sense of smell and taste. She was obviously becoming aware that my presence was defiling the beautiful ambiance of her home.

"Um—can you smell anything?" she asked.

"No, except your coffee and perhaps a trace of exotic herbs from your pantry."

"Pantry?"

"Yes, it's the sort of word they have in romance books about this type of house. I'm trying to become a romantic novelist, maybe with an historical flavour you see."

She exposed her lovely incisors, lateral incisors and canines such was the width of what I mistook for a smile. At the same time, she put her hand to her mouth and choked a little. A wave of shame crashed over me as she proceeded to gag and retch helplessly. I put down my colour-coordinated coffee cup, waved and retreated from the house without a formal farewell. Within a few minutes I was back at the wheel and heading for the Southleigh sewage farm to pump out. In my emotional turmoil and hurried departure, I had seated myself awkwardly and I admit, despite the blinking spy camera, I did make an extensive scrotal adjustment. Sometimes a man just has to respect his own bodily needs.

As I pumped out this beautiful woman's excrement into the sewage beds, I re-gathered my thoughts. How could I apologize? How could I excuse myself to that vision of loveliness that had briefly stood before me? I was a man with full-body halitosis whom no one would ever want. No one except Betty Black. I pulled out my phone and started to delete her pleas and threats. There were promises of a life together in her villa in Cyprus, allegations of bestiality and incest, threats of prison for rape, accusations of psychological abuse, offers of sexual pleasure, photos of her intimate charms and assurances of love and devotion. Inwardly I sighed. Maybe if I played her game there could be a life for me with her? My gut instinct was that she would kill me or that I would kill her, or that we could form a mutual suicide-pact lunch and eat it in heaven. I scanned the overnight list of forty-seven unanswered calls. I knew that somewhere in the shadows, somewhere beneath the earth's crust, a volcano, earthquake or both— called Betty—were building. As I deleted the message memory, more blocked material poured in. A sense of doom darkened my mood as I took a call from the office. It was the foreman.

"Get in here Sparrow—fuck knows what you've done but a customer's been on the phone. H.R. want to talk to you before we respond. Then you're on the bin truck for the rest of the day. That prick Swampy's gone down with contagious impetigo of his bollocks, from scratching himself I suspect."

"Wilco, wing commander," I answered.

I parked up and sauntered to the office. Jean the H.R. commissar was pacing the floor.

"The CEO of Siliconia has been on the line. These people are mega important Sparrow. These people are the controllers of the world. That man invented the chip which Sackman-Platinum bank used to buy America. His company invented the digital Viagra App for ultimate phone-sex."

"He had that look about him. We discussed prime number sequencing," I replied.

"That's why we all hate you, Sparrow, all your Radio Four shit."

"Well, what did he want?"

"He said that you had distressed his ex-wife and that he needed your phone number."

"It was the smell of the suck-out that upset her. She's a classical trombonist. She told me she needs to take deep breaths and she does have a big chest."

"Why are people at that level going to talk to you, Sparrow?"

"Because we were discussing the Siegfried's Funeral March in C-Minor from Wagner's Ring Cycle. It is a trombone masterpiece."

I should point out that one of my great joys in life was to stimulate the foreman's boiling hatred of me. I was always happy to sacrifice any truth in pursuit of war. He took a step closer, his fist clenched.

"You fucking object—,"

I shot him a cheeky smirk and did a little shimmy of the shoulders from my old boxing days. The message got through.

"We'll apologize for your behaviour and provide the gentleman with your phone number," said Jean.

The foreman cleared his throat as if to spit.

"Get out on the bin truck—there's two guys in the cab waiting. I'm going to download your cab camera, Sparrow, so you'd better be hoping I don't spot any infringements."

"Up your ass."

I didn't wait to gauge his reaction and went to the bin truck. Two young fit-looking guys in bright-green reflective clothing were arguing loudly in a foreign tongue. It sounded Slavic.

"I'm guessing you're not the Romanians?" I asked.

"Fuck you driver. We piss on you. We are Czechs. We are Slavs."

"Ah—it's just that we're waiting for a bus from Romania."

"We kill them. They Latins."

"A lot of people don't know that my friends. Indeed yes, their language is a neglected Eastern Romance tongue with many words deriving from military Rome."

"How you say—let's go. We work, we finish. Tonight, we clean office and drive Uber car."

For the rest of the day I shunted and toiled clearing the domestic bin waste of Southleigh. I ended my day, tipping out at the land-fill site with my most consistent of friends—rats and seagulls. The two Czech guys were total grafters, just hired in for the day from an agency. These were the type of men who could become the life force of *Poober*. For a moment I allowed myself to dream of the destruction of Interglobe Effluents. My revolutionary concept could destroy them and a mob of free self-adjusting, non-corporate men would burrow for pennies in the sludge of our society's consumption.

I parked up the bin truck, sluiced myself in Dettol disinfectant and headed for the time clock in the office. I was surprised to see almost a crowd of clerical staff still there at 6pm.

Simon Blanchwhistle clapped his hands ironically as I walked in. He pointed to a television monitor set up in the centre of the open plan space.

"I've asked everyone to stay to show them how *not* to be an Interglobe representative. We've downloaded your cab video and I want everyone to see what type of man you are."

"Why don't you fuck yourself." I said calmly.

"We require you watch the evidence."

I shrugged and faced the screen. I was driving away from Silicon Palais at about 8.30am. I knew what was coming. The BBC radio 4 Today programme was running a feature on social mobility. I'd stopped and was sitting in my seat. I raised my buttocks, broke wind with classical trombone resonance and shamelessly readjusted the alignment of my genitals in my loose underpants. As I withdrew my hand from my clothing I waved it in front of my nose. The camera microphone picked up my mumbled comment.

"Christ, you could chew that," I said.

A couple of office girls and Alexana, a bearded guy who was in mid-gender transition, ran sobbing from the room. The external cab camera showed my location as stationary in traffic at the junction with Chestnut Avenue. The footage ended. There were groans of disgust all around the room.

The foreman expressed the group opinion.

"This is the man who tunes every channel on his radio to BBC Radio 4, Classic FM and Radio 3. This is a man who sets himself above you with his poetry competitions and Latin quotations. Every day women denounce him to Interglobe Effluents as a rapist and child sex offender."

"One woman denounces me," I offered.

"That junction where these filthy acts were committed is adjacent to schools and Southleigh University. Children and mothers with babes were visible on the video footage," concluded the foreman.

Jean the H.R. woman dismissed all the staff.

"Interglobe is sorry to have inflicted this on you. Trained counsellors will be made available to any victims to develop coping strategies. But, our reputation is everything. We must be seen to act in the public interest and have zero tolerance. Just remember in your own conduct that every aspect and activity of Interglobe Effluents is filmed and recorded. For now, be proud of yourselves as survivors of this offender."

"Stuff your kangaroo court," I shouted.

A strident female voice arose from the mob.

"Hear that, from his own mouth? Kangaroos? Hear that? Rolf Harris, he's like that Australian Rolf Harris,"

Thankfully no one had had the forethought to bring a length of rope.

"Hand in everything. You're finished. We'll pay you up tonight and that's the end of you," said the depot manager.

I stripped off my Guantanamo overalls. Underneath I had a pub-quiz Guinness T shirt and my elastically challenged Y-fronts. No one spoke. I had my driver CPC card, Heavy Goods License, Tachometer card and my Aldi steel-toecap boots. As I stepped out, I raised a leg and let rip a rooping stunner. I heard Jean scream.

"Steak and kidney with onions. Gets me every time." I said.

And so, my career ended. I walked the two miles to Sewage Farm Cottage in my underwear without a care in the world. In fact, without anything in the world. Now I could really focus on my personal development as a writer. I was ready for romance.

12 CHAPTER TWELVE

I'd just walked in to Roz's house when I noticed my phone ringing from a number which wasn't Betty Black.

"Sparrow here."

"Um—I'm Michelle, the woman at Silicon Palais."

All of my emotional follicles went into spasm. Her voice was honey, warm sun and kindness.

"It was good to chat over coffee. I wanted to talk to you about Siegfried's funeral," I said.

Immediately she tuned to my meaning.

"The march in c-minor. Are you a Wagnerian?"

"I'm a *trombonophile*. The Salvation Army used to play in my street when I was a kid. I grew up believing God operated on a slide principal because he could change his mind halfway through wherever he was headed."

"I'd never seen things that way. Can God do that?"

"I'd give up the prayers if you don't think so."

There was a moment of silence which I used to reproach myself for my hideously simplistic regurgitation of *Teach Yourself Philosophy*.

"My ex-husband asks if you can meet with him and a couple of his colleagues here tomorrow, after work?"

"I'm free any time—Interglobe Effluents fired me."

"I'm so sorry, what did you do?"

"I broke company rules about control of the vehicle. We're all on camera and they feel my attention was compromised. I'm a serial offender but I don't want to start our relationship by looking like a complete loser. They accused me of comforting my testicles with twenty-two tons of semi-solids in my tank."

"Few women or men would want that sort of thing."

"I'm sorry, you make me so nervous. I've never had a conversation with a beautiful woman who's got a central kitchen island and frogs in her personal pond."

"Thanks for the *beautiful*. I won't have for much longer, I'll soon be just like you."

"Surely you'll have fully elasticated underwear?"

"I'll get my divorce lawyers to cover that. Up until now we've just been talking about houses and pensions."

"I'm sorry to hear that your relationship hasn't worked out. I've been through similar experiences but I'm still in single figures."

"It's hard living with a trombonist, particularly if they don't write computer code."

"I'm a code-free zone."

"Since you're available why don't you come over for a working lunch with the team? Everyone seems really excited about *Poober*."

"That'd be marvelous, madam, I've never been to a business lunch."

"Call me Michelle, please."

"It's difficult—you could be a Radio 4-person, someone I could never approach. I've only ever seen people like you driving Range Rovers into Waitrose."

"Just do it Oscar. Let's say one o'clock."

That evening I ordered pizza, while Roz got out her guitar, smoked some weed and serenaded me with her sixties anthem to sewage farms, "Blowing In The Wind", her loose dentures adding percussion. Man; her long swaying hair and Joan Baez warble took me to Woodstock on a stuffed-crust meat-feast vibe.

As I awoke the next morning three things were clear. The wind had shifted to the southwest and the house shared the same ambiance as the sewage beds. Secondly, this was the first day of the rest of my life. This was the decks cleared for action, new start, no regrets, attack-the-world-and-make-it-work-for-you day, that all the self-help books had predicted. Thirdly, a crazy woman dressed in a posh outfit and camel overcoat was hitting the outside porch door with such force that it was bound to break. Then it broke. I ran to the door.

"You think you're clever, you think you've hidden yourself. You've tasted the sweet fruit of these lips and think you can throw me aside and ignore my calls and messages? Why can't you see what I'm offering you?"

She was crying and sobbing. I felt a surge of sympathy and reached out for her shoulder. Her teeth sank deep into my wrist.

"Bastard. Bastard! How I loathe myself for degrading myself with a turd-monkey."

She started to pound her own face with her fists.

"Betty, do you think you may have behavioural issues?"

She stopped and stared at me. Her face was red and beginning to swell over both eyes as if she had boxed at least three rounds.

"That's it—blame it all on me. See what you've done. You had me put in the cells and now you're going to get the same."

I could see the potential outcome of my situation.

"You did all that yourself, I saw you," said Roz from behind me.

"So, who's this hag? Is this where you ejaculate your deformed seed rather than accept my love?"

Roz stepped past me and pushed her back.

"Piss off, you vile cow. If you come back here, you'll risk a hammer through your skull."

She spoke with a chilling stillness that clearly hit a target. Betty moved back, lifted her skirt to reveal her café-crème lace-enhanced pubis, poked out her tongue, turned and walked to a new-looking VW Polo. I watched her drive away and began to assess the broken pane of glass.

"I'm so sorry, Roz. I'll measure it up and fix it."

"I know you will, Oscar. You've either got to go to the police, shag her, or kill her. The police won't do anything."

"That just leaves murder or sex and I'm only licensed for heavy trucks and buses."

She nodded and reached out to push back my hair with a spontaneous sense of compassion. It was a simple human act which instantly dissolved my habitual flippancy in the face of injustice and disaster. We went indoors and drank a coffee.

"I'm going to have to ask you to move on, Oscar. I can't be doing with this aggro. I like a smoke and Spike deals a bit of crystal for a few friends. She's a cop-magnet and we don't need it."

"What am I going to do now?"

"You need to get her off your back. You must have something pretty impressive down there?"

"I'm a love machine Roz, but she's never had the pleasure."

"She senses it. A woman can detect that inner-wildness."

"Can you?"

"You ain't that bad. All that poetry and classical music stuff makes you a kind of thinking-woman's Neanderthal."

"When do you want me out?"

"You're OK for tonight. Spike is here and he'll just cut her throat if she shows up. I'm not suggesting it, but he's the sort of man who could solve your issue. I've got a suspicion he fancies her."

"I'll bear that in mind."

"You know, we could be close friends one day," she continued while adjusting her dentures. "If Spike were to help you out with your problem and that woman was, let's say—dead, for instance. He's only an occasional companion to me and I appreciate upstanding masculine company."

I liked her. I'd never considered a love affair with a toothless woman of seventy-six. Ever since my encounter at Silicon Palais with the culinary angel of Kitchen Island, all other women had blended into a colourless oestrogen broth. I knew I could never look at another woman again.

"You deserve a better man, Roz."

"Well I know that, but you have to eat what's on your plate," she answered, locking me in a surprisingly strong embrace.

I smiled, not wanting to offend her.

"Let's see how things shape up Roz, I'm still young and trying to get a start in life."

We separated and I fixed the door. I had no car and I needed to get to my business lunch appointment. I walked to the council household waste tip where I knew the guys, to see if they had any bikes. Half an hour later I was on my way with a 70's-style Raleigh Chopper. For now, I was a focused executive and nothing was going to get in my way.

13 CHAPTER THIRTEEN

I leaned my bike against a hedge, noting a Porsche Carrera, Range Rover Vogue, Maserati Granturismo and a Mercedes S-500 already lined up. I pulled the doorbell chain and somewhere deep inside the mock- Georgian style Silicon Palais I heard it sound. Subliminally I think I must have expected a maid because when the door opened I almost fell to the ground.

"Oscar, how lovely." said Michelle.

She wore a deep blue, low-cut dress with red stiletto heels. Her cream bolero jacket still allowed breathing space for her lady credentials. She was beautifully made up to accentuate her blue eyes and soft red lips. Even Ricardo di Napoli couldn't have pulled a woman like this. I stepped into the hall, wishing I'd brought some means of blowing my nose. I sniffed. And sniffed. She smiled and handed me a cube-shaped box of Marks and Spencer tissues from a table bearing an Ormolu glass-domed mantel clock that I recalled from *A Bluffer's Guide To Culture.*

"I'm in training so I cycled. Usually I carry a bog roll."

"I love cycling myself. Come through to the library. The boys are still in a meeting about other aspects of the business."

I followed her, catching some fine perfume and unable not to notice her feminine sway. We passed across a marbled hallway and through high double doors into a parquet-floored library. Many books looked like priceless leather-bound first editions. On the central dark oak table were scattered some more familiar items very similar to my own collection. I picked up *Sold To The Greek Tycoon*.

"I wonder what this could be about?" I said in an attempt to sound superior and sophisticated.

"It's about love and sex, like Barnum was about circus and entertainment. There's a type of person whose intellectual self-importance is based on mockery of love sex and brash entertainment. I'm not one of them."

I did a double take. Her lovely face was offering me a warm open smile. No one, no one, no one had ever spoken to me in such a way.

"There's a magnificent brash absurdity in Wagner. George Bernard Shaw plays the disingenuous common man in mocking his genius. If you fail to comprehend the objective scale of something, one is forced to measure it against the self. The critic merely reveals the poverty and shallowness of their own imagination."

"Fuck me Oscar—where did you hear that mouthful?"

"I made it up. I thought it sounded clever—you know Melvin Bragg meets Andrew Marr."

"Did you believe what you said?"

"I don't know what I believe until I say it. I read alone in lorry cabs. I've no forum in which to spread the chaotic tapestry of my mispronounced confusions. I'm like the Bayeux Tapestry by Salvador Dali. I want you to know I'm an eleven plus failure and have no social entitlement to leave the enclosure of my allotted life status."

Michelle stared at me open mouthed. Even her molars were perfect, her tongue pink and moist. I wanted to worship at this shrine to feminine allure quite possibly involving clothing removal and bodily knowledge. I tried not expose my religious conversion and distracted her by picking up another book. It was a *Honeysuck Romance* but I guessed, translated into French, under the title *Pour Une Unique Nuit d'Amour*. I glanced down the first page.

"These stories love fashion photographers and glitzy cosmetic type businesses," I said.

"You read French?"

"*Oui, un peu—et vous?*" I replied with proto-erotic lounge lizard eyebrow waggling. She giggled.

"Oscar—how do you know French?"

"I drove trucks in Europe. I heard Edith Piaf on Radio 4 and bought her greatest hits. Then it was simply a matter of sitting with a dictionary. How did you learn?"

"School and working there in marketing. You seem to have a very good accent."

"Edith Piaf was very French you know. Some say she overdid the foreign angle."

"Who said that?"

"Americans—they didn't buy the black dress and the songs about suicides in squalid gas-filled rooms."

"*Les amants d'un jour*," she said.

I stared at her. I'd never met anyone who knew the Edith Piaf miserable death songbook. I found her eyes on mine but didn't look away.

"We have a lot in common—except my career in sewage."

"Wagner, France, cycling and romance novels it seems."

"We should cycle to Paris and go to the opera together," I suggested.

She frowned. But she didn't say no.

The doorbell rang.

"Ah, that'll be Connor Bryanston. He's the company president. He's a brilliant mind and he's so excited about *Poober, Shit'Appens* and *Just Shit*."

I accompanied her back to the hallway. On the gravel outside I could see a chauffeur-driven Bentley Continental. A gentleman of about sixty had entered and had a young female on either arm. He exchanged European-style air kisses with Michelle.

"I believe you know Katasha and this is Tia. She's come over from Romania for me to try out, as an intern."

We all shook hands and introduced ourselves. Connor gripped my hand and fixed me with a dominant big-bizz executive gaze.

"We've got to keep this secret, Sparrow. There's competitors out there who would grab something like this."

"I understand, sir. My secret is safe with me."

"Take me through to the meeting will you, Michelle. I've got some grubby little Irishman who sells drain lifters coming in a minute. He won't be in on the main discussion. Keep an eye out for him."

I noted that Connor Bryanston appeared to operate by issuing proclamations and instructions. I found myself grinning at his two young companions. I noted quickly that they had different forms of self-presentation. Katasha wore fashion-style tight jogging bottoms, a pink sporty hoody and very exotic Nike trainers. Her fair hair sprouted from girlie bunches. Tia on the other hand wore a tight sequinned black mini skirt, impossible patent strappy stilettos and a plunging red blouse. Her shining hair was jet black and hung to her uplifted and separated mammary glands.

"I go to toilet," said Katasha.

I stood attempting to keep my eyes on Tia's perfectly made up face. Her mood seemed petulant.

"That woman, that stinking woman—she is prostitute," she said in a wonderful accent.

"I see. A lot of people are unaware of Romanian history," I said.

"They are filthy Latins," said Katasha as she returned.

"I use toilet now, if there no bad smell," said Tia, clacking away.

Katasha reached out and took my hand to reinforce her sincerity.

"That woman—that painted bitch, she is prostitute," she said in a Slavic cadence.

I was beginning to understand globalization and the wider aspects of the free movement of labour. Tia returned as the doorbell sounded and I was glad to excuse myself from the pre-fight eyeballing between the two super models. I opened the door to a man in bicycle clips and holding a bright yellow bike with a basket on the front in one hand and a long-handled gulley lifter in the other.

"Kelly—Sean Kelly's the name," he said in Irish.

"You sell drain lifters?"

"Ah, be Jaysus—it's a bugger being famous wherever you go."

He stepped in wheeling the bike and looked at the two young women.

"Christ—I've seen more meat on a Waitrose meringue. I don't expect you young ladies open holes for a living."

Before anyone could answer, Michelle returned. The Irishman propped the handlebars of his bike against the glass dome of the Ormolu clock. We followed her through to the magnificent dining room with a twenty-seater walnut inlaid table. Old master-style paintings decorated the room which was lit by a crystal chandelier the size of a large inverted Christmas tree. There were a dozen big-bizz types already set up with laptops, folders and bottles of middle-class mineral water. I seated myself opposite Michelle. A side table was laid out with some sort of food that I'd never seen before. She seemed to note my uncertainty.

"There's black radish and caviar with hoisin duck wraps,"

"Are those virgin fish eggs? I've never liked swallowing semen. I'm the same with olive oil," said Kelly.

All the men in the room and the rival super models stared at him in cold silence. I started to laugh, followed by Michelle. Connor Bryanston gave a theatrical sigh.

"Let's get started."

"The boys only do humour as computer code," explained our hostess to Sean Kelly.

"Code? You wouldn't say that if you'd ever had an accidental mouthful of cod spunk."

The afternoon droned on. This was my first ever meeting and I vowed to make it my last. At least I knew now why all the important executives in taxis were so miserable. I spent the time looking at Michelle simply because her lovely face made me happy. She didn't have model type bones or that anorexic junkie arrogance so beloved of glossy magazines. She had a clear day sunniness that burned its woman-prettiness into your soul and tended to give rise to spontaneous manly stirrings. I guessed she was about fifteen years my junior.

When called upon I gave an account of the daily operation of the sewage business. Connor Bryanston had one single focus.

"So, an unskilled guy with a gulley lifter and a set of drain rods could deal with two thirds of domestic or light industrial overflow type calls?"

"Yes, but it's a bit kind of third world," I said.

"I wasn't thinking about being that advanced," he answered. "Now Kelly, what can we do about the price of your lifters if we looked at buying five thousand?"

"Well, I could put the price up because that would mean disturbing my weekend."

Connor Bryanston looked theatrically to heaven and spoke to whatever God he perceived.

"I mean what discount could we obtain?"

Sean Kelly looked up to the same spot in the heavens and put his hand to his forehead.

"Wait, wait—the big guy's got out his envelope and pencil. No sorry sir, he says fuck off."

Once again Michelle and I disgraced ourselves by giggling.

"We'll look at your proposals Kelly."

"I'll hold the production line."

With that the guy re-adjusted his cycle clips and strode from the room. My guess was that we wouldn't see him again. Even through the boredom I was learning a lot about business.

"We can buy that crap in China or maybe Bangladesh for pennies," added Bryanston. "I've ordered a couple online to copy-cat the design."

Comrades, whether you're with me as a writer or someone with some other dream, take note of what has just happened. Kelly respected himself and his own life. Always have a sense of your own worth. This world is full of exhausted fools racing each other to the bottom on price. Authors—some may advise you to give your books away as a means of getting exposure. There's an audience out there for free books and plenty of writers to feed them. Oscar Sparrow has never sucked shit for free.

By evening the masterplan had been formulated. Thousands of operatives would keep a lifter and rods in their cars. They could be out with a girl or boyfriend or even at church or mosque when a blockage call came in. The nearest would scoop the contract. If two operators wanted the same job, they could bid lower and lower against each other. A smaller number of more specialized operatives would lease suck-trucks. They would have special epaulettes shaped like golden turds and be called *Super-Poobers*. The lower level guys would call them in if need be. Just when I thought it was all over, Connor Bryanston stunned the room.

"Gentlemen, it remains for us at Siliconia to complete the software to give this fantastic new platform to the defecating and urinating world of mindless consumers. I've already committed a small army of Romanians to the project and registered the copyright for all the business logos with titles and grabbed all the web site domain names. We'll be ready in a few days. Guys like us are *not* grease monkeys or tool shop money grubbers. This morning I spoke to a good friend who is CEO of Interglobe Effluents. He will launch the suck-truck leasing business in exchange for a seat on the Siliconia board with bonuses. As we speak they're planning to offer self-employment opportunities or redundancy. I've already sold the whole package to a Sackman-Platinum private equity offshoot for eighty million pounds. We've dipped in, sucked out the low hanging gold and left the shitty end of the stick to people better qualified."

"You mean guys like me," I said.

"Sparrow, I'm giving you the chance to suck yourself."

"A lot of those trucks are clapped out and the guys will need finance"

"The CEO knows that. Sackman will finance the truck leasing. This is a dream come true. He's looking at a cool million in his pocket. This is the app' and platform business world and *Poober* is a big job. OK let's vote. All in favour of the deal?"

All the suits went for it except Nigel, Michelle's ex.

"I think we could have taken it further and developed the premium areas such as *Just Shit,* the dietary analysis option for the holistically anal household," he explained.

"It's small change but Sackman-Platinum sold that as a sub-franchise to *Cornfake,* that culty, organic vegan business. We picked up half a mil' and there's an outfit going to sell the smearing sticks and sample pots. We would have needed months to develop it and we all know there's no money in making or doing. Everyone: this deal does not close until we deliver the software. Total secrecy you understand."

In a strange way I'd enjoyed the afternoon. I had seen the inside of big-bizz and dynamic dealing. I felt privileged and knew that one day my insights would be bonded into best sellers. Everyone was in the hallway pretending not to notice the development of a hissing cat fight between the young ladies in their rival languages. Connor Bryanston held out his elbows and they dutifully snapped to their positions. The door swung open to reveal the Bentley with a smashed windscreen and an enormous rip in the cabriolet roof. The chauffeur, still in his grey peaked hat was holding a house brick and trembling.

"Sir, a brick came out of the sky. All I heard was a woman with a growling voice shouting "Fuck you—you've ruined my life." Then a car squealed away.

Bryanston looked at the other parked cars.

"I'll take the Range Rover. I've made you all rich so get on and sort out the mess. Looks like this is a rough area. Good job Siliconia is selling the place. Come on, who's got the keys?" said Bryanston.

One of the executives who'd been at the meeting offered his keys to the chauffeur with an obsequious grovel. A minute later Connor Bryanston had been swept away. The unsaddled international vice president got a ride in the Mercedes and there was nothing left but the darkening dusk, Michelle, me and the calling crows in the oak trees.

"One of those birds must have heard that stitch up deal and shat a brick," I said.

"Who could have done it?"

I looked into her blue eyes and shook my head with a sigh.

"Michelle, do you want to know? If you want to know I'll tell you. It's not your problem but it follows me and there's no reason why you should care."

"I care," she said not taking her eyes from mine.

14 CHAPTER FOURTEEN

I'd never had a friend. It was a great regret to me that my genetic programming and nibbled X-chromosome forced me to conceive my meeting with Michelle as presenting far more delicious possibilities. Why turn a gorgeous sexual woman into a neutralized friend when you can boast about your gas barbecue to anyone? However, telling Michelle about my history with Betty Black enabled me to virtue-signal myself as a gentle and harmless soul unlikely to pose a threat to her feminine purity. I slipped into my wolf suit and she undid the top button of her red hooded cloak.

Comrade writers and artists, I'll leave Oscar to his disingenuous droning about his sufferings to the beautiful and attentive Michelle, and for a moment return to our core purpose. You are reading this book to pursue your dream of being a number one best-seller. Maybe you are trembling before your first ever blank page? Maybe you are reading your twenty-eighth rejection letter or e mail? At the point where this story began, I had written seventeen literary novels and several poetry collections. I used to work on a three-to-one system. It would take me three times longer to write a book than it would for the controllers of the universe to reject it. I'd settled happily into this rhythm over a forty-year period. I believed in myself and what I had to say about working class life. No one in the elite was impressed.

We are all brothers and sisters in the quest although wispy

sensitive poets have homicidal tendencies towards other poets and, are to be avoided. Essentially, as Betty herself pointed out, poetry is boring shit but nobody wants to admit it. Many Poets, except me of course, despise all poems other than their own. Few individuals who describe themselves as poets have ever bought a poetry book. On the other hand, we novelists extensively read the genre we are trying to write.

There is a further category of intellectual writer who produces Literary Fiction. We all know about them because they win prestigious prizes and get interviewed on the BBC. To be this kind of writer you need talent, courage, friends, contacts and a private income. Farcical, quirky self-help books about sewage drivers are unlikely to find a publisher. No one would believe a story like that. Here's the top news ever in the world. If you're the sort of person who, against all the odds and outrage, has the courage to adjust your own genitals when there is need, you're the sort of person who can write the book YOU want and get it out there. This is my pledge to you.

For us, the great mass of keyboard clones, we need to stop using the word Book and substitute the word Product. We need to stop the using the term Recognition of Talent and substitute the terms Search Engine Optimization and Marketing. Yes, this is the truth and there are legions of gurus and high priests out there to help you and sell you their plans, programmes, podcasts, video courses, week-end seminars and of course self-help books. Many of them offer very good advice. Be aware that what is hot today, is stone cold tomorrow, in a business often dictated by the will-o'-the-wisp Amazon algorithms. By the time the latest hottest guru has his book of truth out there, some Amazonian geek or self-learning algorithm has skewed the maths into some other shape. In a minute I'm going back to Oscar's struggles to become a best-selling romance writer for women. The very existence of such a market throws an oblique spotlight on modern ideas of gender relations. My only advice is to write for living imperfect people, not the virtue-signalling avatars of social media with their PC synthetic attitudes. There's plenty of liberal cake-baking kitten lovers on Facebook who don't tell you they read my books one handed because their other hand is busy. The steps I took got me to where I wanted to

be in many senses. Stick with my evolving tale and you'll be able to follow me down the rabbit hole of rodent dreams, to a place where the tunnels are all triangular to accommodate the shoulder-to-waist ratio of Ricardo di Napoli.

Michelle blinked in silence as I concluded the story of my life ending in the smashed-up quarter-of-a-million-pound Bentley being loaded onto a recovery truck outside the window.

"So, what do you intend to do about her?"

"I'll have to go to the police, but I can't prove she threw that brick."

"Isn't it a crime in itself to be a stalker?"

"I don't know. I can understand passionate love and obsession. Sometimes you meet someone who finds a reservoir of visceral emotion inside you. Someone like Nikolai, Ricardo or Francesco can open that window to a woman."

"Yes, I often stand at my window waiting for a passing serenader. I find these books are a more reliable source,"

"It's unusual for any woman to bother with a sewage pumper."

"She doesn't see the excrement worker with his hose in his hands—she sees the poet."

"I'm an ex-poet. I'm training to be a romantic novelist."

I watched her face. I could see she was wondering if I were perhaps a buffoon or a trickster.

"How do you train to be an author?"

"I'm reading *The Gold in Your Gutter,* which has all the inside information. I'm reading romance extensively. They have a lot of sexy billionaire widowers and car accidents. The convoy of limousines and predatory tow trucks is like a herd of grey whales under sustained attack from orcas."

She started to laugh. I knew she wasn't taking me seriously.

"Oscar, I don't think the ladies who write these books see the world with the same similes and metaphors as you."

"Well, of course not. Our couplings have male and female threads."

"Exactly—how the hell are you going to see life from the inside of a woman?"

I smiled and waggled my eyebrows, not wishing to suggest anything that could distress a lady with a kitchen island and a cuckoo clock coffee machine.

"Obviously I'd have to create a pen name and maybe conduct some research to get the feel of the female ambiance."

"I take it you're not attached?" she asked.

"No, except for my admirer."

She stood up and flicked back her long blonde hair.

"Kids'll be in soon. Where do you go from here Oscar?"

"Employment agency and the police station."

"Keep me posted. I'll update you with any news of *Poober*. I'm sure the boys will want to run some technical stuff past you."

I stood up, realising that my worn camouflage trousers were still tucked into my odd socks. I brought my eyes back to hers and then to her lips. My arm ached to lift my hand to touch her face. I flicked a question into that blue heaven of her soul. I knew we were at the frontier of a pre-snog moment. Border guards raised their guns. I had no passport to enter this land but why had no one opened fire before now? I gave her a look of sophisticated yet barely contained molten passion, in the style of Ricardo di Napoli.

"Are you OK?" she asked.

"Of course."

"It's just that you were pulling a strange face."

"No—it's the caviar and black radish, I think I made a pig of myself."

The moment was lost. She accompanied me to the door and wandered across her driveway as I mounted my Chopper bike. I could see her amusement.

"Would you ride that to Paris with me?"

"For the city of love, I would carry it. For you I would fly on it, like with you as ET."

"I'm not sure how to take that but it could be a great trip," she answered as she turned and went indoors.

"ET had lovely big blue eyes," I called to her back.

I pedalled away knowing what I had to do and doubting that I would. My main concern was that Betty would attack Silicon Palais again. I was fairly sure that the police didn't offer third-party preventive custody even if you paid as a private patient. It had grown dark and all the vehicles had lights on. As a safety-conscious citizen I rode on the pavement to prevent an accident. I decided to cruise by Betty's house simply out of curiosity and also to confirm the details of her car so I could spot its approach. Number forty-six Great Western Drive was a smart semi-detached, neo classical mock-gothic late period Wimpey house on a new development. On the drive was a blue VW Polo. I noted the number and pedalled on calmly. As I turned the corner into Benny Hill Knoll, I perceived a police vehicle matching my speed on the road beside me. A muscular and clearly witty young man with a thigh sized forearm spoke to me through the window.

"Oi! Radar man—is that your bike?"

"What?" was my lightning viperish riposte.

"Radar—bit too dark to see without lights, innit?"

"Radar saved Britain from the Nazis and was instrumental in the location of the Bismark battleship in 1941," I added.

I kept riding, uncertain how I could maintain the radar conversational gambit without moving on to speed cameras.

"Just stop, all right. Do you know the fine for no lights on a bike?"

"No, but I offer the stated case defence as in Regina v Lamplighter."

"Stop. Just bloody stop."

I duly stopped as a sculpted, uniformed steroid experiment strode up to me.

"Aren't you that weirdo from the fishing lake woods?"

"I hope you're not anglerphobic officer."

"You're a gobby fucking idiot. You're a loner and there's something creepy about you. Why are you round here anyway? You ain't from anywhere nice like this are you?"

I sized him up and decided he was not a person of natural compassion. He'd made the mistake of telling me what he was thinking. I decided not to tell him the truth.

"Just out for a little healthy ride. The NHS is overburdened by too many obese elderly, with complex chronic issues. That nice Minister of Health is very concerned about it."

"You're going to get locked up in a minute. Where did you get that bike?"

"From the council waste tip this morning."

He grunted and examined my machine before calling in to his controller for a check of stolen bikes. I caught the response.

"Nothing—no Raleigh Choppers since 1982."

"ET rode on a BMX officer. You couldn't give Choppers away back then."

"1982—what are you, some kind of history freak?"

"I remember that year since it was my divorce and we went to see ET at the movies in the afternoon to get the most out our bus ticket."

I began to wonder if ET was going to be a feature of my life from now on. For sure blue eyes were going to be big. The officer took my details, ordered me to push the bike and left me to my freedom. I waited until he had disappeared and rode on. As I approached the sewage farm cottage, I saw Spike nailing a large sheet of plywood to the front bay window. I knew—I just knew. On the doorstep was a bin bag.

"Kill the bitch, shag the bitch, or I will," he said.

"I'm sorry mate. I'm so sorry."

"You heard what I said."

His answer was cold and sincere. There's guys you don't joke with.

"Did anyone see it?"

"Roz saw a champagne bottle as it hit her between the eyes. She'll be out of hospital in the morning."

I picked up my bin bag and wobbled away on the bike. It was pointless to suggest the police in view of the substance issues at the cottage. I thought about starving refugees in Bangladesh and soldiers in Afghanistan. It cheered me up.

15 CHAPTER FIFTEEN

Comrade writers, the closing lines above are not a joke. Everything is relative. If you are going to look for an agent and or publisher, every rejection will seem like a bitter blow. It is not. If you are going to self-publish you will be exhausted by marketing algorithms and humiliated by your sales rankings. My poetry only has to climb past four and a half million other titles to hit number one. Wherever you are headed YOU NEED A GOAL AND A CLEAR STRATEGY.

I needed a goal and a clear strategy. Homeless, unemployed and alone with no direction, carrying my life's total in a bin bag, I wondered what Donald Trump would have done? I'd read his book and was ready to deal and make it art. Was it permissible to pray to The Donald? I looked west and mumbled a few words. I felt a deal had closed. It was a beautiful thing. I wobbled the Chopper into the municipal recreation ground and sat on a bench. It was drizzling and cold. I switched on my phone. In an instant it began to fill with texts, missed calls and voicemails. I listened to the most recent. Her harsh rasp was unnerving even to a man of my courage and fortitude.

"I've beaten you hands down. You're on the run so keep running. You stole my pride and self-respect and thought you could walk away. Keep running 'til you crawl, big man."

Her continuing presence in my life was troubling. I didn't have the funds to consider a contract killing and I had no inclination for D.I.Y. A new call was coming in but not from her number.

"Oscar—old mate—is that you?"

"Is that you Donald?" I asked.

"Who? Nah—it's Swampy off the bin lorries. Look, the Yanks have got the Theodore Roosevelt and escorts anchored in the Solent."

"She's one of the Nimitz Class carriers, well over a hundred thousand tons. Her nickname is Big Stick," I answered.

"Fuck me Oscar—you've done one pub quiz too many."

"Aren't you off sick with contagious impetigo?"

"Exactly. Don't mean I can't do a little bit on the side. A mate of mine works for ASS."

"Associated Suction Services?"

"Yeah. They've got the deal for handling the sewage from her bilges. They want two experienced blokes on the quay for a couple of nights to suck off the tanker. I know you're out of work and it's cash in hand, twenty-five quid an hour."

"I'm up for it but I've got no wheels."

"I'll pick you up, where you living?"

"Recreation ground."

"See you in ten."

And so, my future was secured. I'd have a lorry cab for shelter during the night and a wedge of cash. Was it possible that The Donald himself had sent that carrier battle group to save me? I looked once more to the west and muttered a silent Amen.

I loaded my bike and sat in Swampy's filthy Citroen Berlingo wondering if his contagious gonads had touched my seat. All the same I was grateful as we waited, gutting down our Burger King *Flame Grilled Whopper* meals. Once the truck arrived it was hard work dragging long pipes and keeping the suction end clear of compressed excrement, condoms, tampons, wet wipes and fatbergs. Such items are the pumper's curse and like birds of a feather they sure stick together. I ran loads back and forth to the treatment plant and hauled hoses through an exhausting cold, wet night. By dawn I was feeling my fifty-seven years. We had shifted fifty thousand gallons of Uncle Sam's foul water and sewage. I felt like Leonardo da Vinci stepping back in self-congratulation from the Mona Lisa. A guy paid us out in cash and gave us the nod for the job again that night. I was on top of the world. I'd done my work well and people wanted me. Swampy dropped me off at a run-down hotel in the poor end of Seaborough. We arranged to meet at the same corner that night.

The place was a mess. Everyone wanted en-suite these days and the building dated from the 1930s. The site was up for sale and you could rent rooms for the week. I handed the guy £150 and moved in. Once again, I'd survived and advanced. Even more importantly—nobody knew where I was. I knew I needed to shower. I sagged onto the bed and slept.

I awoke to find my phone jammed with the usual conflict of hate, shame, love and guilt which is the mortar between the thrown house bricks of desire. There were two missed calls from Michelle. I called her number.

"Oscar, Connor Bryanston needs to consult you about drain rod quantities and maximum lengths of operation. He'll be here at two thirty pm. Could you drop by?"

Talking to billionaires about drain rods wasn't my dream afternoon. Playing cuckoo clock coffee with Michelle was another matter. I had an hour to clean up and pedal my Chopper towards what I was beginning to believe was my destiny. On arrival I noted that the big boss had come in his two-seater Ferrari 480 Spider. Michelle opened the door and led me through to the grand dining room where he had set up headquarters. The female I recalled as Katasha sat by his side, stroking his bald head and adjusting his comb-over. I shook their hands and couldn't resist asking after the other young lady.

"No Tia today?"

Katasha gave a stage spit.

"Prostitute!"

"These girls are so competitive but fighting for your place is what you need in a team. Tia is on a mission to visit all my homes, bar-code all my possessions and draw up an inventory so I know where things are. She's moved on to California today," said Connor Bryanston. "Now, Sparrow—we need to draw up the final design for the *Poober* operative's kit. A standard pack of drain rods will reach thirty feet but is that enough?"

I knew the answer, but no one impressed as a consultant by appearing too hasty. It was a wonderful feeling to be among clean successful people who valued my input. I leaned back stroking my chin.

"For your regular estate-type house yes, but for detached properties set well back from the road, you might need a few more. Most blockages will clear using the plunger and the hydraulic properties of the water. Tree roots invade old ceramic sewers and you'll need to worm them out."

"You're a professor, sir—this is priceless information. I'm thinking then two packs of Screw Fix rods. I can get them at twenty quid and market the kit to the operatives for a hundred."

"You could," I replied shaking my head. Obviously when you're a billionaire you squeeze every last penny from every deal.

"Now, Sparrow—the outfit taking over *Poober* are Wall Street bankers. The only thing they know about shit is wrapping it up and selling it to each other as gold. The app will need instruction videos and I've designated you to work with Michelle getting that together."

I did a double take across the table at her. What the hell was this?

"I'm engaged on a project for the US Navy at present."

"Fantastic, what is it?" she asked.

"I'm sucking off sailors. It's amazing what they produce."

"You are disgusting old man," said Katasha.

I ignored her remark and grinned at Michelle who was shaking her head almost sadly.

"You know Oscar, when you were talking professionally about drain rods just now I was impressed by your seriousness. You're not actually sucking off sailors, are you?"

"No, but I always talk seriously about drain rods, it's only too easy to offend their dignity with flippancy and cheap toilet humour."

"And what about your own dignity?"

Her manner had become quite stern, as if she cared. Clearly there was an uncharted sea that swelled around Kitchen Island. She cared about me as a human being. This would take a lot of absorption.

"My dignity is that of a working man's toil."

"OK, Sparrow—Michelle will fill you in. We'll need videos on using the drain lifters and rodding techniques. Get on with it and we'll sort you out for money."

To be frank I felt honoured enough merely to be selected as a super star of the effluent world.

"Sir, had you considered subscribing to Drain Trader magazine? It's the bible of contractors involved in the business."

Connor Bryanston flapped his hand with impatience.

"Detail, detail, I'm a leader and creator. Just get a subscription and brief me on what I need to know. Keep in mind that we're slapping this package together and passing it on. The software tests should conclude tonight. A source inside Sackman-Platinum tells me they've already honed it up a bit and flogged it on to the Russians as a money-laundering front. Bottom line—do the min scoop the max. That's good advice Sparrow and I learned that making my first million. And, just realize I'm giving you that experience for free." He stood and planted a patronizing hand on my shoulder. "Good man. Now, get the show together and report back by this time tomorrow."

It didn't seem worth explaining that I didn't work for him and that I would be labouring all night on the docks.

"You are disgusting old man," said Katasha as she passed by. I found her hard to like. I remained seated as the room emptied. Off stage there was yelling and strangled cries of rage. I knew, you know. I already knew.

"Who left the gates open? Look at my Ferrari."

Connor Bryanston was pacing the driveway kicking at the gravel and sending gurgling cries of rage into the darkening sky. I took a quick glance at the car. Every panel and all the glass had been attacked, I guessed with a hammer. Michelle had opened the gates when I'd arrived but neither of us had closed them. I needed to act. I looked at her and pleaded with her not to reveal my secret.

"I'll fix it for good tonight," I said to her from the corner of my mouth. She replied with a similar yet beautiful jailbird mouth twist.

"That would be helpful I feel."

I watched in awe as a catatonic billionaire raged against some unknown factor of the universe that wasn't subject to his will. I affected a long struggle to tuck my trousers into my socks. I looked around for my Raleigh Chopper. It had gone. It had gone.

The passion of billionaires is nothing to that of a pauper who has lost everything.

"You can fix your Ferrari, but someone's pinched my bike," I said, trying to form a bond of victimhood with him.

"Fuck off—stuff your fucking stupid bike."

"I was merely expressing empathy."

"Look I've lost my Bentley and now my Ferrari. You've lost

some dead-beat piece of shit."

"I knew you'd understand and offer empathy, sir."

A Rolls Royce Phantom hurtled into the drive. Connor Bryanston and Katasha were swallowed up inside as it spun wheels, showering us with gravel as they roared away. I sighed and looked at Michelle. She seemed close to tears. I was only too aware that the unprotected comforting of tearful women could lead to unwanted pregnancy.

"I'm so sorry."

"You didn't go to the police did you?"

"What could I go with?"

"The truth?"

"That old stuff—they've got far better products these days."

For a moment she stared at me.

"Sometimes you're an utter twat. This is serious Oscar."

I sighed, knowing she was right.

"I know and I promise you I'll fix it."

"How?"

"The police—who else? I can't conjure up an assassin like a hell's angel on crystal who'll murder for fun."

She reached out and took my hand.

"I feel for you. Your life seems dreadful."

"All my own work ma'am, say it myself as I shouldn't."

"I'll take you home. What's it like in that cottage at the sewage farm?"

I remembered that she only knew my story up to the previous day. I just couldn't tell her the latest chapter.

"I'm meeting an associate in town. He's giving me a ride to our joint NATO exercise with the American navy. You can just drop me in Underfield Way. I'll dine before he turns up."

"Dine how?"

"KFC—a finger lickin' family bucket. It surrounds me with an aura of nuclear heterosexual inclusion and memories of childhood party vomiting."

"You have a personality fabricated from synthetic fabrications," she said with an irresistible loveliness.

"You can take the post-modern out of the man but you can't take the simulacrum out of the coleslaw," I replied with a well-practised double back flip surrealist bathos.

Michelle was laughing or crying. I swept her into my fifty-seven-year cask-conditioned arms.

"I love you. You've given meaning to my life and shown me respect. I would die for you," I said casually.

"What the fuck?" she answered searching for my tainted wrinkled lips with her own sweet fruit of fem-flesh. We bulldozed and obliterated the pre-snog cliché. Tanker loads of skilfully structured creative writing degree modules lay mixed with death rasping metaphors in the gravel of her driveway. I held her, feeling the woman of her. God, what a joy unmodified X-chromosomes are to a man.

"I'm sorry—declarations of love can repel," I said.

"Who could it repel?"

"Those who fear risk. Those who don't crave the pain of joy."

"What the hell are you, Sparrow?"

"I'm the Poet Lorry-Park."

We kissed again as equals, despite her kitchen island, personal frog pond and my pressing need for scrotal adjustment. There was nothing now but her. I was prepared to gamble everything. I decided to wait until I actually had something in life, to confide my level of commitment.

"I'll give you a lift,"

"You already have," I riposted with a swift personal rearrangement.

Her eyes drew out my being as if I were an ocean evaporating into the longing and merciless physics of a hot blue-sky day. Then we kissed the kiss that would hold our souls for ever in the hands of the other.

No jokes.

No fiction.

No going back.

16 CHAPTER SIXTEEN

Comrades, fellow translators of love into the language of the bus queue, the standing only train and the lonely vacuum of the broken hearted, never ever abandon your sheep to the wolves of cynical disdain. If you can exaggerate your intensity of love, then it is not love. Remember how it is to fall in love and for fuck's sake—give it the utter max and still you will fall defeated by its power to define itself beyond your finest online thesaurus.

I sat in the window of the junction corner KFC. I spotted the blue VW Polo at the traffic lights, Betty Black at the wheel. I spotted my Raleigh Chopper on the folded-down back seat. I realized she was playing the old Mafia tactic of holding a hostage as collateral. I'd guessed she might have followed us but at least she didn't know exactly where I was living. The traffic moved on and I remained seated licking my fingers. I couldn't risk a further attack on Silicon Palais, since Michelle would be there without an heroic warrior at her side. I needed to work and I had no time before Swampy would come to pick me up. I hesitated for a moment before I placed a fateful call.

"Spike—it's Oscar."

"Man, you're a chick-magnet,"

"There's dissolved sex pheromones in foul-waste water."

"That bitch ain't so bad man. She was waving one hell of a pussy before she threw the Champagne bottles."

"A girl often needs foreplay before she lets loose. Look Spike I need her stopped. Can you follow her tonight and call the police if she starts some trouble?"

"Where's she going to go?"

"A big house called Silicon Palais out of town near Shillingsworth."

"What's at the house?"

"Just a girlfriend of mine."

"Hey man—you've always got a hand down your front. You've got some power shower down there boy."

I let him think he was doing a favour for a cool big-dicked guy. There was no reason why he should help me except that he had few friends and I'd helped him fix his bike a few times. Just maybe he would kill her or give her some hot-biker sex action.

"OK man, I'll cruise past her house and hang out a bit."

"Thanks mate. If ever I can do anything for you. Don't get involved with her. Any aggro call the police, OK?"

"It'll be a pleasure. Just get me some of your sex-magnet shit."

"I'll drop some round. Stay safe and call me with any news."

I slid into Swampy's Berlingo clutching what was left in my KFC family bucket. He had a pot of antibiotic cream on the dashboard and took the chance to reach down and rub some into his balls.

"How's your impetigo?" I asked, watching where he put his hand next.

"Vile mate but life's shit anyway."

He dipped into my family bucket and grabbed a southern fried hot wing. I was beginning to like his existential nihilism and he'd done me a massive favour in getting me some well-paid work. We cruised down to the docks and worked the night away hauling hoses and sucking off the American fleet. We shared the rest of the KFC and Swampy's cheese sandwiches as a cold buffet. I had a full belly, money, a place to live and a beautiful woman in my heart. There were issues of dietary fibre but maybe this was the pinnacle of my life? But yet I had a dream to fulfil.

A writer is someone who writes and so far the page was bare.

I awoke remembering that Connor Bryanston had commanded

Michelle and me to produce training videos for the *Poober* app. ASS suction had paid me off in cash and for once in my life I had a small amount of capital. I checked and double-checked my phone. There were a few messages from the previous evening. The final one read.

"If you ever get your bike back sniff the seat, pervert."

My surmise was that Betty had taken up cycling. But why had the guns fallen silent? There was nothing from Spike. It was like Christmas day on the M25 motorway. It couldn't last but all the same I hummed Battle of Britain Spitfire music in the shower. For now, maybe I could go out without fear.

I walked the three miles to Silicon Palais. I organised my route to pass a B&Q hardware store in order to purchase a set of drain rods.

"Do you want the sweep's brush attachment?" asked a lady assistant in her eighties.

"No—I'm only dealing with a bit of writer's block," I replied anxious to build my internal self-esteem platform as a novelist.

The lady answered in a wobbly sit-com voice.

"I blame that bloody double-quilted myself. We just had newspaper."

I marched on, rods rifle-like on shoulder, marvelling at the rich tapestry of life unified by our shared history of drainage. Michelle herself opened the door. She was radiant with burnished skin and beautiful make-up. She wore a cream blouse and black pencil skirt. Her heels looked unsuitable for manhole ladders.

"*Poober* at your service, ma'am—can you show me your access opening?" I quipped.

She half frowned but with a crooked grin.

"Oscar, you have some sort of permanent pantomime going on in your head."

"Oh no I haven't."

"Stop it please."

"What if I see someone behind you?"

"If you really see someone behind me yes, call out."

"OK—I'll get everyone to join in."

"Coffee?"

I wised up and settled down to my imitation of a normal mentality. She fixed me an *espresso doppio* from the cuckoo clock machine.

"Where's the film crew?" I asked.

"Hah—Connor Bryanston believes in the direct gig approach. You lift and rod. I film and speak. I've got a decent camera and sound kit."

"Wow—you'd be a rave in the drainage world. Not many rodders look or dress like you."

"There's been a feminist revolution, Oscar."

"Not in the sewers where I hang out."

"Women are blocked by invisible glass ceilings in every walk of life."

"Maybe that's why there weren't any beautiful women hauling back-breaking lengths of sewage hose all night on the dock."

I could tell she was balancing my political incorrectness against my reference to her beauty. She opted to stay silent with parted lips while I took her in my arms and kissed her. No alarm bells sounded. No Harvey Weinstein effigies fell from the ceiling on neck ropes. Could it be that a man and a woman could still do the men and women things without arrest? I was still very cautious. I set the kiss episode aside as if it had been an extra shot of organic fair-trade brown sugar from the ceramic bowl with matching spoon on Kitchen Island.

"No unexpected bricks or missiles overnight?" I asked with a studied calmness.

"No, did you murder her?"

"Yes, it was lucky I had a clean license to kill. MI6 gives you six penalty points for a murder."

"Your panto is showing again, Oscar."

I looked into her blue eyes. Behind her through the kitchen window I saw a delivery guy waving a drain lifter.

"He's behind you," I said.

She sighed with exasperation as I went to the door and signed for the consignment. Essentially it was a beautifully formed bright-yellow lever about three feet long. There was also a large trolley-type device for lifting heavy manholes.

"Take one. Lights music action," she said.

As tender love developed, I lifted manholes on her property while she filmed my technique. In the afternoon we went out on location where I lifted several gulleys in public streets. We finished our day with a continuous pan shot of me assembling lengths of sewer rods and demonstrating how to use a worm to clear compacted obstructions. As the sun set that evening, her eyes met mine over an open inspection pit. I knew that soon we would physically express our emotional passion.

"I love a scene in *Les Miserables* where Jean Valjean gets swept through the sewers," she said.

"You mean as he escapes from Javert with Marius when the revolution fails?"

"You know it?"

"I dreamed a dream of Vic Hugo," I sang.

"Panto alert, Oscar!"

"I take it you've read the book?" I countered.

"Have you?"

"Yes, but only in French."

"Why the hell did you do that?"

"I thought it might impress a woman one day and I wanted to compliment my understanding of French miz-lit. I'd spent six months reading Zola's *Germinal* you see."

"He was a great friend of Cezanne wasn't he?"

"And a champion of the impressionists. I've always wanted to go to Paris and the Musée d'Orsay."

"Why don't you?"

"Someone stole my bike."

"Get another."

"Only if it's a tandem to take both of us. I would suggest a pantomime horse, but I don't want to set off your alarm system."

OK let's stop there. There was inappropriate kissing involving a beautiful woman and an old man with a drain lifter. We dined on gourmet porcini mushrooms, slices of quince, bat wing paté with beer-battered follicles of veal in a burgundy and shallot sauce. The whole affair was completed with a tossed salad of hand-picked organic walnut and lamb's lettuce with real hill-farmed lamb and a teasing vinaigrette of balsamic bumble bee honey and Armagnac liqueur. This was the first time I'd tasted a Waitrose ready meal. We were two social strata divided by supermarkets yet united in excrement.

During our encounter her seven children had returned to the house, changed into *lederhosen* or *trachtenmoden* to perform a Von Trapp Edelweiss for me in the marbled hall. A stunningly lovely girl in the springtime of her beauty played a grand piano while Michelle added a trombone solo. While their innocent little voices and rasping brass, lilt along the mountainsides, we'll leave them and return to our best-seller quest.

Comrades and scribe-buddies let us see what we have learned. You will have noticed my highly cultured references to the classic works of Zola and Hugo and my pretentious claims to have read them. If you want to be writer you do not have time because you don't have the literary luck to work as a sewage driver. These guys wrote great stories. GREAT STORIES. So, watch the movies. From now on whenever you see a soap or a classic, look look and look again at the story. Trouble not yourselves about plagiarism. Borrow, twist and return. No one will know. This is your orchard to harvest and movies are low hanging fruit.

On a personal note you will see a reference to Michelle's children. You will not see or hear much of them. They are talented and beautiful children with perfect pitch and a wardrobe of Austrian costumes. They have their own lives and the right not to be mired by this true fictional tale of love, tandem cycling and sexual debauchery. Fiction is not the truth. It is an account of true events fabricated from the most compelling and entertaining lies.

I felt quite tearful as the music ended.
"You can see that my priority is my children," she said.
"I hadn't realised you were a Catholic."
"Neither has the Pope."
"Are you in the provisional wing of the Catholic Church?"
"I'm not in any church—I'm just fertile."
"And enthusiastic?"
"My youngest is six, there's some stuff you can't do alone."
Lo, I sensed an abhorred vacuum in the universe as big as the virgin's womb.
"I believe Nature takes an uncompromising stance on negative pressure voids," I suggested.
"You mean I might be gagging for it?"
"I mean you present as a fulsome child of nature."

"I've never met anyone like you," we said in tandem.

"The children will be in bed by ten."

"I might be able to help. I could dress as a monster and frighten them to bed earlier."

"Maybe you could swing by tomorrow and we could edit the video? I've got a quiet place you could write or research your romance story."

Since only four of the children remained in the room crying for food, I felt almost alone and drew her to me in a smouldering embrace.

"Until our lips and souls can unite once more," I said.

Angelic Austrian children's voices cried out.

"Yuk! that's gross."

I strode from the house, a man floating on an alpine cloud of romantic love. A crowd of private tutors of music, language and mathematics were queuing for admission. This was the world I had only ever heard on BBC Radio 4 or glimpsed in the posh Sunday supplements. I resolved to carry hand soap, tissues and a jar of organic capers from that moment on.

17 CHAPTER SEVENTEEN

To be frank I was happy to get away. As the day had worn on I had become concerned about the silence. Several times I called Spike. The first time the phone had made a strange sound like a long beep. After that there had been only his voicemail box. I sent him a text but no response came back. I walked back into town, knowing that my evening meal just had to address my dietary fibre issues. I opted for a Dominos veggie pizza and strolled back to the hotel. I spotted my Raleigh Chopper bike leaning against the wall. An old cardboard box lid was jammed in the back wheel. I read a message scrawled in black marker pen.

"Hot sniff-zone, pervert. Get some of what you ain't getting my jazzed-up poet asshole."

You know, there was something almost great about her work. It turned over anger like a plough slicking and rolling its rich tilth into a symmetry of parallel furrows. It was as if rage could boil into a richer essence of itself to catch its glints of cutting flint as the merciless blade curled it aside, open to the gaze of black crows. Sometimes I had dreamed of being a poet. Every time editors had had nightmares about my poetry. Now I was a romantic novelist. I tried to figure out why she'd returned the bike. My guess was that she wanted to bug me by letting me know she knew where I was. But why hadn't she simply called me? And just how did she know where I was? Only two people knew—Swampy and Spike.

I let the question mature, fairly certain that Swampy couldn't be in the frame. Still there was silence. My mind replayed all the submarine movies I'd ever watched with the ship untroubled on the surface and the evil U-boat captain shouting "Fire One" as he folded back the handles of his periscope. I wandered into the hotel where the desk guy was watching the local TV news. The background was a fire truck with an anorexic posh-voiced female presenter throwing copies of Roget's thesaurus onto the flames.

"The raging fire at dawn brought the whole street to attention. Dozens of families, some with terrified pets and sweet tiny babies were evacuated to the church hall in the Square where the reverend Berkley Nightingale arranged hot soup and a sung mass. Meanwhile hero fire-fighters battled into the white-hot inferno to extinguish the boiling conflagration."

The report switched to the local fire chief.

"It's too early to give you a cause. At present it looks as if there are no casualties as the occupant's vehicle is not at the venue. The lady is a well-respected London barrister who often works early and late."

"Could it be arson, could a crazed criminal be on the loose in Great Western Drive? Could Southleigh be at the mercy of a homicidal madman?" asked the reporter, trying to reassure the public.

"We will be working with the police and other agencies to establish the cause."

"Could there be a link to a terrorist cell or a radicalised loner scheming and bomb making under the noses of unsuspecting and innocent neighbours?"

The fire chief shook his head in exasperation.

"We are ruling nothing in or out."

As the reporter closed and the studio anchor turned to sport I felt faint. I walked on through to my room without comment and slumped down on the bed, my heart pounding and my mouth dry. Just what the hell had happened? Should I go to the police? Would the police be coming for me? The bike had reappeared during the afternoon and no body had been found at the house. I needed to talk to Spike and if anyone knew where he was, it would be Roz. I took a deep breath and walked out to the Raleigh Chopper. I went directly to where it had been leaning against the outer porch door frame. I went exactly to the same spot. OK—there was no bike. There was no bike. I went back in and spoke to the African guy on the desk.

"Did you see anyone take my bike?"

"I ain't seen no bike."

"The bike that was leaning against the door frame."

"I ain't see no bike."

I gathered that my question was not within his operational context. There was no bike. I looked around for the cardboard bearing her message but it too had disappeared. There was no bike but at least I knew that she was alive or at least someone involved with her had delivered it. It seemed logical that a passing opportunist thief had it now. I called Spike again but it went straight to voicemail. I needed to know where he was and it was a four mile walk to the cottage at the sewage farm or to his room chez Mr. Singh. I was about to set out when I realized there was a ring of police officers around the hotel and they were closing in. A burly plain-clothes-type was bearing down on me.

"Hands behind your back," he barked.

"I wasn't even thinking of adjusting myself,"

Strong official experienced hands were pulling my wrists backwards as the handcuff ratchets tightened around my wrists.

"How am I going to scratch if I need to? There's genital impetigo in the area," I said, trying to strike up a rapport.

"You're under arrest on suspicion of arson and murder. You don't have to say anything but if you fail to mention something now that you later rely on in court it may be held against you. Do you understand?"

"I want the court to know that I'm relying on you to find my bike and scratch any part of my body by proxy while I'm in handcuffs. I believe these rights are enshrined in the Magna Carta, a copy of which is just up the road in Salisbury Cathedral."

"They told me you were a prick," answered the voice of the law in a broad Hampshire accent. I felt myself almost weightless as the officers swept me towards the waiting prison-style van. Once again I tried to establish a degree of empathy.

"I expect all this is routine to you guys," I quipped. "It's nice of you to carry me since last time I was dragged."

"You weren't a fucking murderer then."

"One must allow for a degree of social mobility, officer. It's good to know I've got a foot on the ladder of deviancy. I slipped off the housing version many years ago."

I found myself in a conversational void on the cold floor of the van. A bin bag hurtled in on top of me. My 1970's clock radio and soup spoon clanked against the Ford Transit metal. I heard the voice of the hotel desk guy.

"You're out of here mate. Fuck off."

"I'll be back," I said in pure Schwarzenegger.

"Boss don't want you back."

The doors slammed.

I resigned myself to my fate as my face bumped on the cold metal and my arms ached behind my back. The ride was harsh and in my view driven by an amateur. I felt I had to help.

"I'm a professional class one HGV driver and I feel the hazard awareness of the chauffeur could do with some instruction. Would it help if I drove?"

"Shut your ugly mug," came the voice of the law.

I allowed my body to respond to the vehicle motion and vomited the Waitrose ready meal onto the officers' feet. An orgy of disgust raged and climaxed above me in the darkness as we came to a stop at the police station. Beer battered veal follicle slime and snot hung from my face as I stood before the desk sergeant.

"Arson and murder—book him, Danno," I offered as an opening comic reference.

"What?" asked a serious looking important man of about twenty-three.

"Hawaii Five-O, 1968. That's where I learned my law. Get me an attorney, I'm taking the fifth amendment."

"Everyone told me you were a prick," he replied.

"Can we just talk about arson and murder? I hate to talk me, me, me all the time."

"Do you need a doctor?"

"I could do with some facial slime control and if I defecate I will be unable to wipe in handcuffs. I will sue the Chief Constable for any long-term sphincter trauma and apply for the 7.30am traumatised victim-of-the-day slot on BBC Radio 4."

The young gentleman listed my sleeping bag, soup spoon and 1970's clock radio and asked me to sign. I was released from the cuffs.

"What about my bin bag?" I asked.

"It's in the bin—cos it's a bin bag," he said in a duh voice.

The surrounding posse of deputies guffawed at his wit. I inflated myself with the gravitas of Jezzer Corbyn on Marxist Momentum acid.

"Where do you keep your possessions sergeant?"

"At home."

"Then restore to me my home," I *quothed* to the uncaring gallery.

"Do you want anyone informed you're here?"

I thought for a moment. There was just one person who could help me.

"Police Constable Jones. She is a lady but she has to pretend to be unisex so as not to offend. She didn't fool me right from the start."

"We'll tell her. I'd be surprised if she doesn't know."

"Am I notorious, infamous or simply a local celebrity?"

"Do you want a lawyer?"

"I only know two top barristers on a personal basis because I have few social connections. Please call either Ms. Betty Black or Mr. Tarquin Montacute. He is a consultant to one of the companies with which I am associated."

I was stripped, handed a white paper one-piece CSI suit and led away to the cells. A thin pale ratty face squinted through the trap in the door facing mine.

"What you in for?" he rasped.

"Murder and arson but I'm not sure in what order."

"Yeah—you got a jail vibe man. Respect brother."

My captors slammed his tiny window of redemption and pushed me into my quarters. It was cold. I wiped my face with bog roll and restored my dignity. I lay down on the concrete ledge and thought of the blue eyes and the kiss of Michelle's lips. The only man truly in prison is the man without a dream.

18 CHAPTER EIGHTEEN

My mobile phone had been seized as evidence. Whatever events were unfolding beyond my cell were out of my control. Clearly Betty's house had burned down and clearly both she and Spike were missing. I felt no malice for the police since such matters were serious. I was more or less certain I was not guilty. The cell door swung open and the burly arresting officer sidled in. I estimated he'd lived forty summers in the police reservation. His jet-black thinning hair had the orange glow of a darkening treatment. I tried to demonstrate my polite and cooperative nature.

"Please could I have the good cop first to warn me that the bad guy is outside if I don't confess?"

"You're some sort of wise-ass. I want you to shut the fuck up and give straight answers."

"That sounds reasonable officer. I'm sorry I mistook you for the bad cop."

"I don't like you Sparrow and asking around a lot of people feel the same way."

"Random polls can be misleading. Statistical curves need experienced analysis."

He sighed and shot me a dark Hollywood tough-guy sneer.

"We're going to interview you under caution."

"Can't it be done over caution, I'm claustrophobic."

The officer grabbed my Theakston's Best Bitter pub-quiz T-shirt and spoke harshly into my face.

"Shut the fuck up. You're in the shit, *geddit*? No more stupid comments."

"I'm getting really worried about the bad cop outside now."

I walked with him to a small room with a table and four chairs. The walls were lined with a sound deadening fibre board. Bolted to the table was a double cassette recording machine.

"Is that there for the steam punk fans?" I asked.

"It's there because that's what there is."

"I think you would find digital technology far better. I might write to your chief as a concerned taxpayer."

I must point out that I was aware that my constant flippancy was irritating the detective. As a young lady carrying a sheaf of papers entered the booth I decided to adopt a different approach on account of her female allure and cool self-confidence. She had lustrous dark hair, a size fourteen womanly form and an ivory complexion.

I offered my hand to shake.

"Oscar Sparrow, ma'am, the Poet Lorry-Park."

She didn't take my hand but looked me in the face with fascinating grey blue eyes.

"I'm Detective Inspector Martina Knight and this is my colleague Detective Sergeant Garth Hardman."

"You're very lovely Inspector. Were it not for my pre-existing fascination with another woman I would write you a poem. In the circumstances I hope you won't mind being the heroine of my next *Milf in the Filth* erotic romance novel?"

The Inspector motioned for me to sit opposite them. I played it straight and listened while they told me my rights and how they were going to record the interview. The show went live and Sergeant Hardman opened the batting.

"Do you wish for a lawyer?"

"Can't they wish for themselves? I wish them well but I think they should stick to stuff like divorces and criminals."

"You are in custody suspected of arson at forty-six Great Western Drive and the murder of Elizabeth, Tamina Boothroyd-Black QC, better known as Betty Black."

"She's an attractive woman with behavioural issues. Do you need me to identify the body?"

"We don't have a body," said Inspector Knight.

"Ah, this is a virtual murder game and my imprisonment will end if I lose my data signal. I was beginning to worry this was all real you know."

"Oscar—let's talk openly," she began in a soft seductive voice, "I know you had more than enough motive to want her out of your life. You abducted or murdered her, torched her house to cover the evidence of the struggle and then used her own car to dispose of the body. The jury will understand what you did. I mean, you're a pathetic womanising loner but she was one hell of a mad bitch and you didn't deserve all that."

"And she stole my bike," I added.

"So that's a confession," bellowed Hardman.

"Of course, why would I cover up the theft of a Raleigh Chopper? It was the first such incident since 1982."

"What's this bike rubbish?"

"Look, I don't want to press charges. She brought it back just before I was arrested."

"Where is it now?"

"It disappeared."

Hardman got the nod from the beautiful, sensitive and fully formed inspector to pursue his line of questioning.

"You're saying that she stole your bike and then brought it back about an hour ago but now it's gone?"

"Exactly. It's such a relief to see you understand."

"So how do you know she stole your bike?"

"I saw it in her car outside the KFC last night."

"So obviously you called the police?"

"You guys have better things to do I'm sure."

I watched the soft yearning lips of Martina Knight as she spoke to me.

"Oscar, a police patrol stopped you in her street the evening before the fire. Why were you there?"

"I just wanted to see the place and make sure I could spot her car."

"You were sizing up the place and her vehicle?"

"Yes."

"Where were you last night?" asked Hardman.

"Sucking off the American fleet on the dock. It was cash job for ASS. I was driving a shuttle tanker to and fro the sewage farm."

"So, you left the dock and could have gone anywhere?"

"No, I was only away for about an hour. Swampy Marsh was with me."

"We spoke to him. He says he's never worked for ASS and he's off sick with genital impetigo so it would be illegal for him to work and not declare it."

Obviously the net had been closing in on me all day. How could they know about Swampy? It was time to beat the rap.

"Inspector Knight, you seem to be the good cop. Betty Black had attacked a house where I was performing some media and consultancy work. I asked a friend, Spike, to keep an eye on her and call the police if she went back there to cause trouble."

The two police officers exchanged glances.

"Could that be Ronny Steele the Hell's Angel and crystal dealer, released last year from Wormwood Scrubbs prison on parole for GBH?"

"He's a biker. I only know him as Spike. They call him that cos he's got that mohawk hairstyle. I don't know his actual name."

Hardman moved in for the kill.

"You asked him to follow her, or what?"

"I haven't got any wheels and I had to work on the dock."

Detective Inspector Knight looked me firmly in the eye. There was a delirious depth of female essence calling me from her soul. I kept my vision of Michelle held up as a shield to block her beauty.

"Oscar, you're saying that you sent this violent drug-dealer round to her house and he agreed just as a favour? Did you not think he might go beyond your request?"

"He's Spike the Bike that's all to me. I think he thought she was attractive because she had shown him her *noo-noo* when she attacked the sewage farm cottage. Secretly I was hoping he'd sort her out."

"Sort her out?" growled Sergeant Hardman.

"Yes, you know sexual penetration but lifted from the merely physical by emotion."

"So, you reported this attack on the cottage?"

"No."

I decided not to mention the reluctance to expose the house to police attention on account of the substances therein.

"So, you paid this Spike to get rid of her?" snapped Hardman.

"I didn't pay him. I just wanted to stop her. I'd lost my job and my home on account of her. It was a desperate idea just to make sure she didn't attack Michelle's house."

"Michelle?" asked Inspector Knight.

"She's a business associate. I'm helping some techies to design a digital platform product."

"What is it?"

"I can't say, I've been sworn to commercial secrecy by a very important billionaire."

Hardman gave me lip curl and sighed.

"Let's recap. Betty Black stalked you and caused you a lot of problems. You were afraid she'd attack your lady friend Michelle so you sent a violent Hell's Angel to deal with her, even by way of a sexual encounter on your behalf. He disappears, she disappears and her house gets torched. You claim she's alive because she stole your bike, brought it back this very evening but when you looked it had gone again."

"You should have been a Tony Blair spin doctor."

"Oscar, Do you have sexual problems such as addiction or compulsive pathological recidivist behaviours?" she asked.

"I imagine you're a criminology graduate—a first for sure,"

"Modern languages but I'm doing it post-grad."

"I could be a really useful case study so if I can help let me know. The commonest recidivist sexual offence is indecent exposure but the most likely precursor to stranger rape is regular burglary."

Hardman gurgled and slammed his fist down on the table.

"Jesus Christ, Sparrow! You're locked up for murder and arson and you're giving the police a lecture on flashers."

"He's right though, Garth."

I beamed at her lovely countenance.

"It's all there in *Understanding your Urges—A Self Help Guide*."

She laughed, almost with a girlish innocence.

"No such book exists Oscar."

"OK—just once I lied and you got me."

"We're going to leave it now and check out some of the things you've said. Write down the address where this Michelle lives. We'll be talking to whoever lives at Sewage Farm Cottage. All your mobile phone data has to be analysed. We'll need you to describe Spike's motorcycle. Interview concluded at 10.14pm."

Hardman clicked off the machine and parcelled up the tapes. There was a lot of writing and signing of forms.

"Inspector I meant what I said about putting you in my book. I'm going to move you to Scotland Yard. You're going to be zapping around the world in a fabulous crime and love story involving a gorgeous boxer."

"Dog or pugilist?"

"You choose."

"You're not a regular guy, Oscar. By the look of your face you've boxed a few rounds."

"Absolutely but your guy will be a winner and a champion. I didn't get this ugly by winning fights."

Hardman led me back to the cell and pushed me in without comment. I made myself comfortable on the concrete ledge and closed my eyes. Michelle's lovely face came to me and I held her. Despite the cold and my hunger, I slept in happiness.

19 CHAPTER NINETEEN

By morning my mood had deteriorated. Fundamentally I was in the shit. I couldn't blame the police because they had a serious fire and two missing people to account for. They could see I had a powerful motive to get rid of her and my account of the phantom bicycle seemed implausible, even to me. One thing really bothered me. The cops had said they'd interviewed Swampy. The only way they could have known about him was if Spike had told them himself or grassed me up anonymously. If I could find out how the police had got to him we would all be on the way to arriving at the truth. It seemed unlikely that the police would want to share such a vital clue. I was confident that the achingly beautiful Inspector Knight would have discarded Swampy's denial of having worked for ASS as self-protection from the tax authorities.

One big question. Why would a regular drug-dealing Hell's Angel on parole for GBH go bad and help the cops against an innocent shit-sucker? While I was turning over these matters in my head, the flap in my cell door opened. A Styrofoam plate and matching cup started to appear. I heard the caress of a soft female voice.

"Breakfast Oscar."

"I hope that's organic wholemeal toast. I have dietary fibre issues." I said as I took the beautifully matched serving set and peered through the grille. It was her, Judy Jones who had taken my statement after the attack at Mr. Singh's lodging house. "It's a great comfort to see a friend, Judy."

"I'm not a friend, I'm just doing jailer duty."

"A man knows who is a friend in his heart. I know friendship would be unprofessional in your situation and with a big riot cop at home."

"You remembered me and what I told you about my life."

"What decent man wouldn't remember you?"

"For a lounge lizard you have the poorest wardrobe I've ever seen."

"I always wanted an all-white suit. Judy—please tell them out there that I'm innocent?"

"I'm not supposed to talk to you about the enquiry."

"I know but you're my only hope. I want you to know I'm going to write you into my new romance story. You'll be immortal."

Her kind wonderfully feminine face broke into a smile.

"Thank you, Oscar. Look, everything against you is circumstantial. I want you to know I don't think you did it. Most people just think you're a complete idiot with one too many pub-quiz T-shirts."

"Who doesn't want to know the height of Big Ben?"

"Detective Sergeant Hardman for one. I'll tell you this, OK: the forensics on the house fire aren't showing an accelerant. Looks like the fire started in the lounge, maybe a naked flame, maybe a cigarette or electrical fire. There's no sign of a body or bodies in the house. I need you to promise you won't let anyone know I've told you that?"

"I promise, Judy. By the way thanks for the ten pounds you left for the book. You're going to get a signed first edition. It'll be priceless once I'm famous."

"I can't wait, Oscar."

She slammed the flap shut and was gone. I turned to my white limp toast and weak tepid tea. At least I had a meal. If they released me I'd have nowhere to go. I raked through my mind wondering where to focus. Then it came to me. Ninety-six metres—Big Ben is ninety-six metres in height. Objective certainties are a comfort in times of doubt.

Comrades and fellow scribes, while the hapless Poet Lorry-Park contemplates his future in his cell, allow me to impart to you a very important feature of the self-publishing business. A

couple of times Oscar has promised people a role in his story. The lesson here is that people really matter. Your fans will matter and these days they want to join in. Michelle and I often run little competitions for a reader to get their name into a story. Secondly if you want to produce a story involving a cop or a clergyman, try to get close to them. I'm not suggesting getting yourself arrested for murder but there is a mass of open source material such as recruitment sites and non-fiction crime stories. If you want to write about a vicar, hang out in the pews. There are blogs, trade publications such as Drain Trader, Pest Control News and forum sites about more or less everything. Lift the manhole of life and enjoy.

Sergeant Garth Hardman filled the door frame of my cell.

"You didn't give any address when you came in. The boss wants you bailed while we pull together all the leads but you have to have a fixed abode."

"If you can provide a broken abode, I'll fix it up myself. There's a wealth of self-help books on DIY."

"You really are a stupid twat."

"I'm a homeless stupid twat."

"So, there's no one and nowhere?"

"Many philosophers and religious gurus would offer that as a definition of freedom but I can see you understand my position."

He stepped out and slammed the door. I could see that for once my own problems coincided with those of Authority. The only friendly face left to me in the world was Michelle, and with her seven children I would never expect her to risk a murder suspect on bail under her roof. In truth I would think less of her as a woman and mother if I was able to coerce her into helping me. Without my phone I had no sense of time. The day was darkening when my cell door opened.

"You've got one chance only to say yes or no. Roz Banks has offered to put you up at Sewage Farm Cottage. If you don't want it you'll be staying in and maybe getting a bail hostel place next week." said Hardman.

"Roz? She wanted me out of her home cos of what Betty did."

"She's cool now, she thinks you killed her or had her killed. She wants to congratulate you."

"How did she know I'm here?"

"If you must know, an officer acting on her own behalf in her own time called round there to see her. Roz came straight down to the station, poor misguided cow."

"Judy Jones, that woman is an angel."

Hardman grunted.

"She's guarded by a huge angry riot cop," I informed him.

I followed him through to the room where I'd been searched and signed in.

"Your clothes have been retained as evidence for forensic tests. You will be required to sign in at the front counter every day between 1800 and 1900 hours." said a uniformed sergeant. I shrugged.

"I just want my bin bag, clock radio, soup spoon and money."

As I walked out into the public waiting area, Roz Banks stood up. Her dog's snout butted my groin. My heart went out to her. The champagne bottle had hit her full in the face. She had stitches in a wound on her forehead and two black eyes.

"You all right, Oscar?" she asked.

I noticed immediately that she had no dentures. She picked up my interest.

"The bottle smashed my teeth mate. I hope someone has fuckin' murdered the evil witch."

"If they have it wasn't anything to do with me. Do you know where Spike is?"

"I know where he ain't and where he ain't going to be."

"Did you fall out?"

"Yeah—you might say there's an empty space in my life," she said as she took my hand.

We walked together hand in hand through the evening streets of Southleigh, she with her mismatched wellingtons, bruised face and me wearing my one-piece, paper scenes-of-crime suit. To any outsider we must have looked bizarre, yet in our own minds we were wrapped in the robes of friendship. Only the lonely know the bitter freedoms of silence and invisibility. I treated us to a monster fish and chip supper with pea fritters and a pot of curry sauce with a battered jumbo sausage for her dog. While we re-heated our feast in the oven, she rolled a joint, got out her guitar and sang me Blowing in the Wind. Sometimes being a chick magnet is frightening.

20 CHAPTER TWENTY

Roz munched happily with her gums.

"So, you don't know what happened with me and Spike then?"

"No, course not."

"You know he was seeing that Betty Black?"

"Are you sure?"

"Yeah. The dog pulled a pair of her knickers out of his leathers."

"Did the dog recognize her scent, he seems a groin specialist?"

"Nah, but I recognized them from her performance out in the road. Then you called him and wanted her watched. I didn't say anything but when he didn't come back I walked round there. His bike was on the drive and they were in there shagging on the floor"

"Did you see them?"

"Yeah. The whole place was set up with candles and they were at it on some kind of witchdoctor rug."

"What did you do?"

"There was a skip up the road. I got half a broken toilet bowl and heaved it through the window."

I had to admire her fire and passion but felt a certain concern about the development of our own friendship.

"Did you tell the police about all this?"

"I didn't mention chucking the crapper through the window but that lovely police girl, Judy Jones, came round and I told her the bastard was up to his nuts in guts with her."

I reflected for a moment. If the police knew the story then a lot of the heat was off me. I was so grateful to Roz but my heart belonged to another woman. At other periods of my life, a woman's senior age and absence of teeth would not have disguised her inherent loveliness. I was in a vulnerable situation with few options. I played for time.

"Can you work out why a top London barrister would take up with a Hell's Angel with a history of violence?"

"Anything beats a shit sucker. My poor deceased husband was a sewer rat so I'm hardened to it."

She scooped up the last of the curry sauce with her finger and gave me a generous Nigella Lawson style wink as she slurped her lips. My mind played a ping pong of deep psychological torment and molten emotions as only ever experienced before by Ricardo di Napoli. Basically, I was in a trap between a toothless nympho geriatric and Hornchester prison, a building which is in fact of considerable architectural interest. It seemed very probable that Roz's half toilet bowl missile had caused the fire but candle-lit sex on a witchdoctor mat is a well-known dangerous sport. Clearly she was a woman of uncontrollable passion and I did owe her for springing me from jail. I thought of Michelle with her band of perfectly pitched angelic children. What a contrast there was between us. There could be no future with someone from a different universe of humanity. With Roz I could have warmth and food and such things are not to be sniffed at, particularly at Sewage Farm cottage. I was only fifty-seven but I knew that soon I would have to concentrate on building a life for myself as a romantic novelist. As I pondered these matters I was aware that the bad local smell was particularly strong. I'd given a battered sausage to the dog and Roz had eaten all the curry sauce and a pea fritter. At first I thought that either the dog, Roz or both had broken wind. Increasingly I caught a peculiar hint of foul water which always accompanies raw effluent. If I hadn't known better I would have said that a main had fractured. Roz had gone through to the kitchen. I heard her open the back door.

"Fucking Jesus—fucking shit," she yelled.

I ran out to see a huge plume of sewage firing thirty feet into the air. The main feed pipe from the town had fractured. I quickly estimated the potential flow from a twenty-four-inch pipe, assuming a normal five-degree slope, could well be about seven thousand gallons per minute. The River Scratchen was nearby. Priceless trout fishing areas and righteous vegan watercress beds were at risk. My mind flashed back to films where hero fire-fighters dashed into buildings to save film stars. I remember some guy who extinguished oil fires, his rugged face illuminated in the flames. I began to wonder if I could run to triumphal music in slow motion like a Hollywood hunk. Although society had rejected me, I was prepared to risk all to save my country, this land of mongrel dogs, Pukka pies and third round of the FA Cup.

Within seconds I was immersed in the struggle. Foul water sewage battered me from all directions like the last moments in the doomed submarine. I tracked back to the nearest isolation point. Through the boiling tempest, I saw it—a twenty-four-inch gate valve set in an overflowing spill containment tank. I knew that only a superman would be able to turn the wheel and save the planet. I went into slow motion handsome mode and with all my force gripped the cruel steel, slowly bringing the emergency under control. My handsome face was set in a rugged and female underwear-dampening grimace. I slumped down in exhaustion, aware that the jetting stream of world threatening raw sewage had ripped off my paper crime scene overall. I heard a shout and pulled myself up naked to receive the laurels and adulation that surely would be mine.

"Fucking get away from there whoever you are," came a voice from somewhere behind a powerful flashlight.

A crowd of Interglobe Effluent workers was pouring from vans parked on the service road. The first scouts reached me as I stood on a concrete wall.

"What the fuck are you doing? You can't trespass on private property."

"The twenty-four-inch main fractured. I rushed in to shut it down and save the galaxy from the *Turdicons*."

"Yeah well Interglobe doesn't need this sort of story so just sod off mate."

"I think the press should know," I said.

"I think some naked pervert ought to shut his mouth," said the leader.

I began to answer but was aware that my feet were slipping on the slime covered wall of the containment tank. The last thing I recalled was the taste of the sewage water as it closed above my head and I sank into the solids at the bottom.

I awoke in the General Hospital. Plastic pipes had been inserted into my nose and a fluid drip tube had been taped to my arm. I was aware of a figure seated on a chair next to my bed.

"How do you feel?" asked a serene female voice.

"Good."

I was aware that my throat was bruised and raw and lifted an aching arm to my neck.

"They had to clear organic material urgently from your mouth at the scene."

I turned to see a vision of paradise.

"Michelle—why are you here?"

"Long story but the police took a statement from me while they had you locked up. They told me they'd taken your phone. We needed you for a few details to get the *Poober* project signed off so I called the station to get a message to you. They told me about the incident."

"I saved the planet from an alien attack by the *Turdicons* you know?"

"They said you'd been trespassing naked. Interglobe Effluents want to press charges and they've banned you from living at the cottage."

"Roz knows what happened. You haven't said why you're here bothering with me."

"The best reasons between people are when you don't have to have a reason."

"Hey, I'm going to put that line in my romance novel."

"Are you serious about doing that?"

"Sure I am, why do you ask?"

"Sometimes you don't seem serious about anything."

"Would you want to dwell seriously on my life to date?"

"Maybe; if I knew the *true* story."

"OK—I made up the *Turdicons* but they are out there. My big question is why would any man leave you?"

"Because *any* man wasn't ever what I wanted."

"He told me it was the trombone."

"Not everyone likes a brassy woman."

"Not every man knows Siegfried's funeral march in c-minor my dear Brunhilde."

A nervous young doctor came in with a clipboard.

"Your oxygen saturation is still a bit low to let you out. You breathed in a lot of fluid, Mr. Sparrow."

"Tell me the truth doc. Will I make it? Will I walk again? Did my navigator eject and evade capture by the reds?"

"You need a Vladimir Putin fantasy calendar Mr. Sparrow. You also need to look after yourself. Your cholesterol is raised and there are indications of dietary fibre issues. I've asked the public health team to do a lifestyle analysis."

"I'll look after him doctor."

I stared at her. How could this lovely being care for me?

"I can't ask you to do that."

"You didn't ask me. Anyway, Siliconia is selling the house. The company bought it as an investment but Nigel and I are divorcing in any case. Connor Bryanston wants the grounds and everything maintained while the place sells, if you're up for it."

"But where do I live?"

"Silicon Palais—there's plenty of rooms."

"You're not afraid of me—that I won't harm your family.?"

"No."

"Just like that?"

"Just like I spoke to PC Judy Jones and Inspector Knight. You're all police checked and you're sound. I'm not saying you're normal because—I don't want to insult you, but you're not normal."

I was very conscious that in a now distant land and time I had kissed her and had she hadn't pulled the pin on my Top Gun ejector seat. I just had to get focused, act sensibly and repay her.

"Stick with me Brunhilde—no mountain top ring of fire is going to hold me back. When do I start?"

21 CHAPTER TWENTY-ONE

Fellow followers of the muse, you've probably been wondering when I would actually pick up a pen and write. The fact is that every step of every day right from your first memory has been a preparation. The writer in you edits, exaggerates and transmogrifies all those thoughts and events which have built you. Fiction is not a memoir. This book itself is an edit of the truth. However, it is the absolute truth about my experiences in getting those number one best-sellers.

The day came when I set out to write my novel. Everyone is different in their approach but once you start it is like the new puppy or as anti-natalist types would say; the baby. You have to forget everything else. You tickle the baby, feed the baby, house train the puppy, walk the puppy. Something far bigger than you has come into your life and will not go away. This is what you do. The world turns on and spins off its loose debris. Your world is that story and the characters who live in it with you. At the end your life will seem a void without them. When I finish a romance novel I know how good or bad it is by how much I miss the characters in my daily life. If you're writing and you get that buzz you're doing good stuff no matter what the world says. The world and its fashions change but that buzz is always the buzz. Never settle for less and your readers will repay you.

Michelle collected me from the hospital. We went directly to the offices of Siliconia where Connor Bryanston reviewed the video footage we'd done with the drain rods and gully lifters.

"This is fantastic. I can see a world on the horizon where most people will do most things as self-employed gig workers. Taxi drivers, journalists, language tutors, truck and bus drivers, drain cleaners, literary agents, teachers, nurses, actors, lawyers and so on. All workers will be competing against each other. The guys on the forest floor will race each other down to the bottom on price and the cheapest and the most desperate will win. These are exciting times for an entrepreneur."

"Any plans for romantic novelists?" I asked.

"No reason why not. As an outsider it looks like a gig job anyway. Now here's the story on *Poober*. It's wrapped up, polished and gone. We pushed it out to Sackman-Platinum and they've sold it on at a mark up to a Russian outfit. We scooped ninety-two million but we agreed to take thirty-one million in commodity future options. All in all, we've done OK but the final take will depend on the Moroccan fig harvest or some crap like that."

It was an education for me to see this guy in action. He never touched a tool, Moroccan fig, or dragged a heavy suction hose. The existence of his world made me sad in a way I couldn't identify. When he'd finished, the girl I knew as Katasha took his arm. A different girl took the other. I guess he saw them as gig workers.

"This is Reka. She is my new Hungarian intern," he explained.

I smiled and shook hands. Already I was sketching out stories about powerless people maybe three or four books ahead.

Comrades, once you commit and label yourself as a novelist/writer that becomes the context of all your interactions.

We drove back to Silicon Palais. Michelle found me a pen and school exercise book. I went to a quiet room on the upper floor where there were fitted carpets and heating. It was far better than the regulation freezing garret. I wrote the title *Punch-Up*. I already had my heroine so the opening was easy. I read aloud this new revelation of my genius.

"Martina Knight left her Metropolitan Police warrant card in her Jeep Wrangler. Here she wasn't a cop. She wasn't a woman. She was a fighter. The acrid perfume of male sweat in the gym sent an unwanted sexual surge to her belly. In the roped ring above her, a glistening, tattooed-male slammed punches into the focus pads of his trainer. She stopped to watch. The boxer had seen her from the corner of his eye and smiled.

"Hey, Martina—you wanna step in with Billy Tempest?"

"You ain't ready for what I got," she answered.

"True, but you ain't a world champ and Billy Tempest's got the belt."

She sucked her teeth.

"Don't give me all that third person shit. There's only room for two in a relationship. Martina Knight calls herself I."

No longer was I a low-life sewage operative. I had become a writer. Inspector Knight would live every breath with me for the next four months. I didn't know it but I'd already made a fundamental mistake. I was writing the book with the characters and story I wanted to write... AND WANTED OTHER PEOPLE TO READ. THERE WASN'T A BOOK LIKE THIS IN THE WORLD. JUST LIKE THE BOOK INSIDE YOU.

If you're looking for an agent or conventional publisher this IS NOT the way to go. My book was a cross-genre mish mash. That doesn't mean I wasn't writing a best-seller; far from it. Just a few days ago I was listening to the new blockbuster audio version of this story narrated by the professional, marvellously fun and talented Roberta Kalina. Here's my take. If you want to get published by other people, study exactly, exactly, EXACTLY, THE PRODUCT they're already producing. If you want to be true to no one but yourself, be true to no one but yourself. Then Michelle Mabelle will shake your hand as a comrade. We can do great things together.

Let me put this another way, from the publisher's point of view because I love those guys. OK—you're a fishmonger. You sell fish. Every Friday you sell extra kippers but on Saturday everyone wants prawns. Then some wise-ass fisherman strolls in and tells you that you need a hybrid kippered shrimp to cover both days. You're a fishmonger—you tell him to fuck off.

It is also time to tell you of my own position as a writer and human being. I had a career as a performance poet and writing through the National Poetry Foundation. I had written shorts for magazines and won a range of writing competitions. I had

written seventeen "literary" novels before I went into genre Romance. All of them were both praised but finally rejected by agents and publishers. I had had many different day jobs including many years as a truck driver—with considerable experience as a shit-sucker. In my younger days I was a boxer, chemical plant worker, pedal rickshaw driver and vehicle mechanic. I've worked in hotel kitchens, slaved as a demolition labourer, sold stuff door to door, run a market stall, operated a bakery oven and stripped the casings off soiled prison mattresses. I've slaughtered poultry and worked one handed off ladders painting high-rise blocks. I view my lived life as no more than an apprenticeship for my real purpose on this earth as a writer.

I turned up at Michelle's door with a life completely de-railed and sullied by a female stalker. All of the actions of Betty Black in this narrative are essentially true. Whilst I play the story for laughs in this work, anyone who has been stalked knows how terrible and tragic such situations can be. For years I had to adopt different names on social media sites and always lived under the threat of some horrid trouble. Every person and case is different but I would urge anyone in such a situation to seek help at once. Once an ex-partner or would be admirer crosses that line go to the police.

GO TO THE POLICE.
YOU ARE NOT MAKING A FUSS.
YOU ARE LIVING IN HELL.
YOU CANNOT PLACATE OR HUMOUR THEM.
GO TO THE POLICE.
YOUR TORMENTOR WILL NOT SEE YOUR PAIN AND ACT WITH WHAT YOU REGARD AS NORMAL COMPASSION.

GO TO THE POLICE.

The chapters grew. As the characters developed on the page and in my own mind I thought less and less about that Frills and Spoons lady I'd heard on BBC Radio 4. The fact was that the characters had started to dictate the book. I tried to beat them into the correct shape to fit the mould but they kept squeezing out like a would be size zero with a taste for wine and pasta. To be honest I have never developed the ruthless dieting and discipline to turn out the exact slimmed down product. *Angsting* about things like "dialogue ratios" can cause serious harm to your mental state.

I decided that since I had become a romantic novelist I needed to get away from the whole sewage scene. I considered signing up as a *Poober* operative but to be frank, the wages were likely to be low and uncertain. I returned to taxi work on a self-employed basis since this allowed the freedom to work on my writing.

I had moved my clock radio, soup spoon and sleeping bag world into Silicon Palais where effectively I became Mellors, the game keeper character in *Lady Chatterley's Lover*. Within three or four months I had learned the children's names and their friends stopped running into the house shrieking that there was a wrinkly vagrant in the garden. I was making progress at playing the triangle and crossing the social class divide into a world of confident educated people who could taste the actual organs in organic guava fruit. As you will recall I had to report daily to the police station and await the outcome of all their enquiries. It seemed that Spike and Betty had disappeared into the ether of time-space. As it stood it was largely assumed by Sergeant Garth Hardman that I was a murderer and that it was only a matter of time before he could close the net around me. During that period, I bought a laptop and used it to post poetry and features on an internet site called *Scribe-a-Vibe*. The format was that writers put up chapters of their work, poems, features and short stories. The idea was that other writers offered praise, advice and opinions about the displayed pieces. One day I had posted a short poem and among the usual gushing praise for my genius was a comment in poem form in a style that I recognized at once. It read:

It ain't Cricket
You smashed my delivery into long grass
And so the grass snake viper
Bites your bat and breaks your balls.
Clever man—you had no maiden over
Fuck your smug defensive stroke,
Prick—no loving crease for you—you're out.

The poet gave her name—Betty Black. I stared at the screen. I checked other work I'd posted and found that every item had been visited by the same poison pen. I won't bore you with the details but the featured work is a guide to the flavour. Two thoughts jumped into my mind. She was alive and even worse, she had found me on the internet. In those days I had little involvement with so-shallow media but everything I was learning about the world of genre romance was telling me that I needed to get a big online presence. Michelle was already busy building a web site and organizing stuff like blogs and book tours. The captain of my fantasy U-boat was yelling *dive dive dive* as I retracted my periscope and headed for the depths.

The next night at the police station I reported my sonar contact with the enemy to Sergeant Hardman.

"Don't prove a thing. You could have put that on there yourself," he said.

"If you knew my style you would note subtle differences in my poetic rhythm. I am the Poet Lorry-Park and my work is quite well known."

"Sparrow—you're the most irritating murdering bastard I've ever met."

"Let not your irritation prevent you from contacting *Scribe-a-Vibe* and tracing the I.P. address of the sender. Then you will be able to locate her whereabouts."

"Do you think I don't know that?"

"I'm only saying what I read in *Forensic Ace Detective Weekly*."

"You make my blood boil, Sparrow."

I could never resist watching Hardman's repressed loathing of me.

"Surprisingly that would be more or less the same temperature as water. It's quite a common quiz question."

"Fine—we'll follow it up."

"We could be friends Sarge," I offered.

"How?"

"I could write you into a book—a block-buster self-help book. You'd be immortal."

"Any other time-wasting suggestions?" he sighed.

"I want to ride my bicycle to Paris with a very beautiful woman but it will be very difficult to report in here every night. Would you notice if I skipped a few days?"

"Yes; and why do you want to go to Paris?"

"I'm researching a book about a hero cop who loses her head to a sexy boxer and snogs him with wet tongues of yearning knicker-busting passion all over Paris."

"Just get out."

Deep down Sergeant Hardman was a good man. He didn't like me and I knew what wound him up. On an artistic level I knew he'd identified my naive trademark style error of excessive emotional description. I knew the next thing he was going to do was to trace Betty Black. I also knew that for my writing career to progress, I was going to have to be someone else. It was time to try out life in the lacy gusset fast lane of fame.

22 CHAPTER TWENTY-TWO

There's something inherently gorgeous about a gusset. The word conveys the soft secrecy of woman. As a carrier of a nibbled X-chromosome wobbling on its one leg, I have always been compelled by the gravity of the universe, into the contemplation of the swath and the joy beyond. These days such open desire for the loveliness of the female is almost criminal. Cast me on your lace-trimmed fires, erect your erections and stretch my neck on a rope braided from silky gussets. Send me home to my creator for so she made me. But, could a manly shit-sucker write from the heart and underwear of a woman?

There is no official ban on males writing romance stories for females. However, as a newbie I knew it would be hard enough to get a publisher deal as a female without adding a further hormonal barrier. The fact was that Betty Black had discovered me on the internet and had already left me jobless and homeless. My old self was dead and could never be revisited. I strode manfully towards Kitchen Island as I entered Silicon Palais.

"Michelle, I need to re-invent myself."

"That's an interesting philosophical idea Oscar. Self-invention poses issues around causality."

"Every schoolboy is aware of the determinist paradox, Michelle. I thought I might start by wearing your underwear and working outwards."

"I have no intention of swapping them for your Y-fronts. Why don't you simply buy some in Marks and Spencer?"

"How did I end up in this bourgeoisie? ASDA does a fair range."

"Fine—but this is the TV drama point where the tortured self-blaming woman tells her man that he owes her an explanation and that they need to talk."

I explained the new situation of Betty's discovery of my online presence.

"So, you're going to adopt a female pen name?"

"It's worse than that. The new world of saturation celebrity means that you have to be ever-present on social media with photos of your dinner and posing with your pets in bikinis."

"What sort of pets wear bikinis?"

"Viral video pets that get you so loved by millions of followers. Just think how fantastic it would have been had my syntax been clearer and *you* actually wore the bikinis yourself to advertise your blockbusters."

"How about a naked tight-rope walk across Wall Street?"

"Michelle, you're a genius—would you really do that for me or even for us?"

"For us?"

"One day I'm going to be massive and I'm cutting you in," I said, realising that I might have proposed marriage.

"There is the little issue of finishing the book."

"I'm on top of it. I need another week."

She smiled at me with genuine warmth. I couldn't believe anyone like her would bother with me.

"I'll do anything to help you," she began, "but I can't use my own name and photo because your writing is a bit physical and I have to think of the children."

"You mean the bit in the gym where Billy Tempest is working his pecs with his weights?"

"I was thinking more of the sun-drenched naked sixty-niner on the open deck of the luxury yacht."

I could see her point even though they had both applied sun-bloc and been tested for sexually transmitted infections. While I was thinking she went to her computer and tapped a few keys. There were pages and pages of women offering their images as models. A few of them even exposed their faces.

"These agencies will sell you the rights to use these shots. We need to choose someone who matches our corporate brand" she explained.

"And what about the name?"

"I don't want anyone to know it's me. I do *not* need school yard mums pointing me out as that woman who writes about puddles of need in the female areas."

"I've never written about puddles of need in the female areas. That must be one of the established greats you've already read."

"Yes—it's not your style. You're more of a burgeoning fluid symphony spilling into the bloom of ecstasy type."

"I'm a poet."

"I still don't want the mums telling their children I'm a debauched porn-monster."

"That may be true but if you're going to pose as someone else it's best to keep your own first name?"

"How so?"

"I read it in *Espionage for Beginners*. The G.R.U. Russian secret police will call out a name as you walk across Red Square to see if you respond. If you've given a false identity you won't react. When you're in the audience with all the intellectuals at the Mann-Booker presentation you need to respond to *Michelle*. If you don't run up and gush you owe it all to your parents or Oprah, the second guy has to go up and get your prize."

"I could live with *Michelle* because it's a common enough name."

"You could be Michelle Sparrow."

"I'm beginning to note a gambit of disguised marriage proposals in your conversation," she said, fixing her blue eyes on mine.

"I'd noticed that too and it's lucky for you that you're not divorced because you might not be able to resist."

I opened my arms to her and held her. How could life have given me such happiness? I could hear the children forming up in the marbled hall in their *trachtenmoden* and *lederhosen* ready for *'The Lonely Goatherd'*.

"Can't they do something different like Lennon and McCartney? I'm sick of Austria," I said.

"Why not indeed. What's your favourite?"

"That's easy, Michelle—ma belle…,"

"That's it Oscar—you're a genius. *Michelle Mabelle*—that's the name."

While she got out her trombone and I searched for my triangle upstairs, I went to the writing room and typed '*Punch-Up by Michelle Mabelle*'. The universe had a new star.

Comrades, these events unfolded a while ago. Since then the world has become even more of a screaming match of so-shallow media. Whatever your take on our society, you must embrace it. If you have committed to being an author, you have offered yourself as a sacrifice to the digital altar. You will need Author Platforms, Facebook pages, Linked in profiles, Twitter accounts and of course personal appearances. You will have to be conscious of your image and your readers at all times. You will be public property and the machine you set in motion must be fed. If you self-publish at least half your time will be internet marketing. If you get a conventional "old fashioned" deal with agents and a publishing house you will have more time to write but often less freedom to write what you want. There will be more of this issue as we progress. Remember guys, this is a self-help book NOT telling you how great life is if you BUY MY BOOK. This is a book about staying sane, being yourself and WRITING A BEST-SELLER. Selling a best-seller is another universe.

So, let's get on with the narrative of Oscar Sparrow's transformation into the romantic novelist Michelle Mabelle. In our enlightened times, it is perfectly accepted that perhaps millions of people are in sexual transition. Oscar's condition is now recognized by the World Health Orgasm as Pre-literary Intermediate Secondary Sexuality, better known as the PISS syndrome. In those darker days many people thought such individuals were merely taking the piss.

I wrote the last lines of the story and repeat them here for your pleasure and to allow you to sense the power of my talent:

"I love you, Martina" he said, spitting his blood-soaked gum shield into the adoring crowd."
"Give it to me hard, Champ," she replied.

Well, that's OK then. It all ended 'H.E.A.' as they say in the

trade. Happy Ever After is a romantic fiction certainty. Lonely drug-addicted freezing unrecognised fashion photographers do not sell books. Beautiful working girl fashion photographers scooped in an erotic whirlwind by billionaires do sell books. The good news is that billionaires have impeccable pecs, lascivious lats and tantalizing tatts. These days never forget to stir in your tattoos. When a modern girl gets what she needs it's not love—it's Tattisfaction. These fashions will evolve for ever and tomorrow the tyranny of the billionaire tattoo may have passed. Ageing tycoons with blurred blue Samoan warrior war art will adorn the mortuary slabs, murdered by contemptuous young fashion nymphs. The quest will be for pierced punk celebrity pecs or minted Mohican millionaires.

The important thing is that you constantly scent the air for change. When I first wrote for magazines, you could get a hit with a window cleaner called Jim. The modern romance reader firstly needs to be dissatisfied—filled with a lust that no regular guy could even dream of understanding or satisfying. The guy next door is total shit—unless he's an undercover billionaire. In a case like that, only a corporate, fashion, real estate or magazine executive has the wiles to uncover him. Bus drivers, office cleaners, street sweepers, fruit pickers and the like, do not have the emotional or physical equipment to survive in the beautiful world of Romance.

It was springtime in Canterbury and the drought of March had been thoroughly pierced for those of a Chaucerian turn of mind. I had now written the first draft of my story. Now I needed to hone it into a masterpiece by doing what Chaucer had done and go on a pilgrimage. In order to gain the exact flavour of my Parisian love scenes between Inspector Martina Knight and Billy Tempest I needed to go to Paris. How could I just write a word like *'café'* on a page and leave it like that? I needed that smell of roasted grains and the scent of chic perfume wafting from the impossibly aloof mademoiselles on *La Rue de Rivoli*. That authenticity would soak into my pages.

My taxi career had developed and I'd purchased a London cab on finance. In order to have quality writing time I was working weekend nightshifts among those of the vomit and violence tendencies. The plastic-seated rubber-floored vehicle was ideal and had the advantage of fencing off the driver from difficult clients or indeed those who felt entitled to non-payment. Several times young gentlemen suggested I could offer them my stash of cash. I always declined with apologies, pointing out that although I understood their desire for my money, I had a powerful desire to retain it.

You will recall that I'd asked Sergeant Hardman for permission to undertake my Parisian research whilst on bail for abduction, arson and murder? Of course, it was his duty to refuse. Dare I skip bail in the name of literature?

I had promised Michelle and the seven children that we would all cycle to Paris. I had spent several winter weeks fixing up an assortment of bicycles. Michelle and I jointly purchased a tandem plus a trailer for the transportation of the trombone, a couple of guitars, a flute and their wardrobe of *Sound of Music* costumes. Owing to the intense beauty of the females most of the other bikes carried cosmetics, hair straighteners and dryers. At last, one Wednesday night in May I reported to the police station, signed on and led the convoy to the Newhaven cross-channel ferry. I was now a suspected capital criminal on the run. The following morning, we landed at Dieppe and headed for Paris. It would not be until the evening that the police dragnet operation would begin. My hope was that Interpol detectives would not be watching obscure cycle routes in Normandy. In my heart I knew I was breaking the law but also knew I was innocent.

Now, this trip has nothing to do with the narrative except of course that I was researching the ambiance of Paris for the central section of *Punch-Up*. The adventure became profoundly significant when I chanced upon an established colossus of literature and artist who ran a Bed and Breakfast establishment at a little French village called *Fairmay le Pissoir*. We arrived exhausted by cycling mid-afternoon to find it closed and populated by a gang of sniggering youths who apparently had never seen nine Lycra-clad people on a rag-tag of bikes with a trombone. Since I was a fugitive from Interpol I didn't offer them an Anglo-Saxon smack in the gob. We found the beautiful manor house where we had booked *Chambre d'hôte* accommodation and wheeled our bikes into a courtyard populated by chickens. Madame was a handsome dark-haired lady in an enveloping canvas apron.

"*Zair is you dinnair*," she explained, grabbing a passing bird and performing a miracle of origami with feathers. Up to six of the children fell to wailing and we whisked them away to lovely rooms where they only managed a subdued run through of a medley of songs from *Oliver* to reflect their mood. Whilst *Le Manoir* was spotless and authentically Gallic in every way, there would be nothing to eat or drink until eight thirty. Although *Fairmay le Pissoir* had a corner shop and a bar, they observed French opening hours and remained closed. We resisted cannibalism but the youngest kept giving us nervous looks.

At last we were called to dinner. As we entered the dining room my eyes were drawn to the walls which were hung with large paintings of naked women, some in thick bright red oil pigment which lent a 3D effect as in Van Gogh. I took a seat under the dripping red triangle of a furry female pubis. It was clear that the artist's model was none other than the lady of the house. While she served a starter of cold, hardened broad beans in brine concentrate, the artist himself entered in smock and floppy hat. He introduced himself.

"*Bonjour les Anglais. Je suis Henri de Pot-Pourri, zee artist and writer. This is my wife Marie de Pot-Pourri.*"

"I am Oscar Sparrow, the Poet Lorry-Park and this is my marketing manager Michelle," I replied.

"And the children?" queried Madame.

Michelle studied their faces and counted them.

"Yes, I think they're with us."

The main dish was the chicken which had been boiled and cut into eleven chunks. I received the parson's nose and one of the feet. Various boiled vegetables floated around in *'La Sauce'* which was like a thin English gravy but without the flavour. It was obvious that the poor fight put up by the bird in the farmyard was on account of its age.

"My wife is a *cordon bleu* in the true tradition of the French country *potager*. This dish is from a recipe of her grandmother."

"I imagine she knew this chicken herself?" said Michelle gnawing the skin from a chicken foot.

"The sauce is a tradition of *Fairmay le Pissoir*. The vegetables are grown in the organic droppings of the forest wild boars."

As we chewed I enquired about our host's writing career.

"Oh yes, I am very well known. My novel *The Vivisection of Juliette* is a science fiction classic."

I reflected upon the red colour of his paintings.

"Is vivisection something that interests you?"

"In the sense that the intellectual practises his enquiries on the living mind."

"But not fitting electrodes into the brains of football supporters to see what they think about the referee?"

"Such things would not interest intellectuals."

He got up and went to a bookshelf. He selected about a dozen books and piled them up in front of me.

"My mind has no limits of power and intelligence. I grew bored with the expression of myself in words. Publishers queued for my manuscripts but the truth is that few readers were worthy of my thoughts."

"I'm writing a book myself," I said.

"Oh yes, what is it?"

"It's romance, a lady cop falls for a boxer."

"This would be a story for the mass of lower people I am thinking."

"That's the plan."

"Very good—how will it be published?"

"Good question – can you offer advice?"

"The cousin of my brother's wife was at the Sorbonne with *Jean Paul Ecrivier*, the director of *Editions Tartuffe*. Over dinner he had once said that he was seeking a true intellectual to expand the minds of the upper-middle classes; these peoples who just needed to stretch a little further in their thinkings. A meeting was arranged and finally I agreed to write him some novels. In truth it was hard to simplify my words and thought sufficiently for such an inferior audience."

Comrades, fellow grovellers before the beauty of words. The above conversation happened in France with a French intellectual. You will note that he actually earned a living by operating a B&B. Those of you who listen to BBC Radio 4 and 3 will have noted intellectuals who are often referred to as 'the novelist' or 'the writer' as if there were only a few of them. (To the BBC the whole trash industry of guys like you and me, not

to mention the e-book scene, does not exist). It is very difficult for a sewage tanker driver to find acceptance as an intellectual or to have a family or contacts in positions of influence with publishers. Having said that, organisations such as the League of Love Writers' Guild and The Society of Scribes are networking platforms and offer the same kind of opportunity. I would advise any aspiring writer to get in there.

But here's the big point. When you meet 'big' writers it's easy to be discouraged. Often they have connections, admiration and social importance whereas your path has been nothing but put-downs and rejections. Being a true intellectual can be a positive block to mass-market success. On the other hand, you might really want to run a B&B.

Big Tip: Look up the websites of writers whom you aspire to be like. Very often they list the groups and societies to which they belong. Being a writer is like being a duck. You know, if it looks like a duck, quacks like a duck... get yourself waddling like a writer and join up!

Our little convoy moved on. On several occasions I had to tell the children that it was impossible to get maximum pedal power whilst crying in pain. I assured them that later in their lives they would love me for sharing my insights into suffering and achievement.

Eventually we arrived at our next scheduled stop, a farm in the little hamlet of *Colon les Carottes*. Of course, the whole village was closed with no one in sight. Here we were served white *Boudin* sausages, which I would describe as a slosh of sloshy pale meat, served with a slosh of white sloshy beans and a mashed slosh of sloshy boiled potatoes. The meal was accompanied by the red-faced agricultural host walking up and down behind the table explaining the process of slosh production.

"Ziss is the tradition of Colon-les Carottes. The pigs feast on the organic acorns of the forest. This is not the Genetically Monsterized meat of the Anglo-Saxons."

The following day we moved on to an industrial estate on the outskirts of Paris. We arrived in cold pouring rain after a ten-mile section of dual-carriageway with horn-blaring heavy trucks. Of course, the *Formule* hotel was closed. A sign on the reinforced barbed wire gate read *Closed until 6pm*. There was a phone number which I called. A gruff individual answered.

"The hotel is closed," I said.

"*Oui, zair is a sign.*"

"We want to check in."

"Yes, you can be first in the queue at six o'clock."

"That's in two hours and I have seven children and slightly fewer bicycles."

"Ah Monsieur, you are a cyclist."

"Yes, *naturellement.*"

"OK, I am a sportsman myself. I am coming."

In a few minutes a large battered Citroen van arrived. A portly guy in a track suit and Nike trainers with a cigarette dangling from his mouth jumped out with a huge snarling Alsatian dog on a chain. The animal sharply butted my groin. The male threat of my pheromones were recognized internationally! He opened the main gate and main doors and ushered us in.

"I am security. There will be staff later."

"Which are our rooms?"

"Anything, anywhere."

We didn't hesitate to spread ourselves through the entire building since whole hotels to oneself come rarely. While hair drying and cosmetic procedures occupied the females I set out for the nearby *Auchan* supermarket. That night we feasted on plastic tubs of Italian pasta, lumps of ready cooked chicken, warm fresh baguette, yoghurt, Babybel cheese and cans of diet Coke. It was delicious and as any French person will tell you, French cuisine is the finest in the world.

In the back of my mind, I was concerned that I was a fugitive from justice and could well be the subject of an Interpol warrant. Michelle's phone was ringing. She listened carefully then handed it to me. I immediately recognized the voice of Detective Inspector Martina Knight.

"What the fuck are you doing Oscar?"

"I'm in Paris researching your love scenes with a world champion boxer."

"You're an utter buffoon. You haven't signed in at the station and now you're in deep trouble."

"Let's work on this together. How can we move forward from here?"

"Look, we know that Betty Black was alive after the fire. Her car number plate was picked up at the Channel Tunnel with her at the wheel?"

"Was my Raleigh Chopper still in the back?"

"You really are a stupid, stupid man. Anyway, if you hadn't run off we would have released you from police bail."

"*C'est la vie*. If Napoleon hadn't turned France into a military dictatorship in 1799, the Revolution of the common people would have failed."

"Listen Oscar. For some reason I'm trusting you. I've taken it upon myself to save your ass and I haven't put out a wanted notice on you. I'm trusting you to get back here and report in."

I could hear the concern and sincerity in her voice.

"I'm truly grateful. All I can do to repay you is to make your name immortal in the annals of erotic detective fiction."

"Just stay out of trouble and get in touch as soon as you're back."

How could I disappoint such a woman? The least I could do was to give her the hottest love ever to burst and explode in the molten female core of a Scotland Yard Inspector.

The caravan cycled triumphantly past the cathedral of Notre Dame into the heart of Paris. In the couple of days that followed, Michelle and I traced the path that Martina and Billy Tempest take in the book. It was his desire to kiss her under every bridge. We took the river boat and performed the scenes as written, distracted only by the cries of disgust and vomiting of the seven children. After each clinch I made careful notes. We'd planned to spend a week in Paris but a trip to *'Glaces de Bernard'*, the world's best and most extortionate ice cream shop, burst our credit cards and we were forced to return to England. Luckily an ad hoc performance of Rogers and Hammerstein classics in *Les Jardins de Luxembourg* netted our return costs. Another of the children was suitably smeared with authentic slime de Paris and sent to do Diablo juggling tricks in a subway to cover our food. The boy done good. As a reward we exposed the children to the pinnacle of French cuisine. We dined on the finest sauce-covered rodents, molluscs and entrails of Europe all the way back to the coast. I barged Celine Dion aside and stood on the prow of the car ferry.

"You will never forget this experience," I intoned to the children in that pompous manner that tall old men in salmon-pink trousers possess.

Years on, the poor souls are still trying. But they can never forget.

The Poet Lorry-Park will never ever wear important-man-in-Waitrose salmon-pink trousers.

23 CHAPTER TWENTY-THREE

The printer spat out the last page of the manuscript. *Punch-Up,* by Michelle Mabelle existed. I went into first-person flashback as if I were writing my first ever commercial magazine story. Should I choose Bill the steady guy at the workshop, or offer my raging follicles to Zarostro, the Latin dance champion of Chipping Sodbury?

Such questions are difficult enough in fiction for Mandy, the launderette service wash maid. As a literary great on the eve of discovery, there were simply too many options. I went to the library at Silicon Palais and took down the *Scribes and Thespians Almanac*—the bible of the scribbling supplicant. There were more literary agents than there are stars in the sky. I saw quickly that few publishers would consider *'unsolicited submissions'*. All roads led back to Frills and Spoons. Once again the voice of that BBC Radio 4 lady came back to me. I learned that *Frills and Spoons* were part of a larger empire called *Honeysuck*. They had many separate formats ranging from Intrigue, Teen, Medical, Historical and so on. The website made it clear that they would accept *'unsolicited submissions'* but that you had to select the correct department. Failure to do so would lead to exile in total darkness. In the end I chose *Honeysuck Inferno* since they favoured hot love over virginal goodness. The troubling thing was that there was nothing about cops or boxers. Maybe in the future there will be a *Honeysuck Gumshield* or *Honeysuck Handcuffs*. If you look at the *Honeysuck* website today you will see pictures and biographies of all their editors. Even back then I realised that these beautiful smart ladies are predominantly well educated with university degrees in publishing, literature, journalism and so on. This is not a criticism since that is their business. You will find no one with a background in late-night cab driving, boxing or trucking. The system was that one sent off the first three chapters and they would then contact you to say if they wanted the rest. However, things were not quite at that stage.

I had written the book by hand and then typed it in two revisions. I felt it was time to ask Michelle to read it. I left her alone in the library and performed my daily tasks of swimming pool management and tending the grounds. Siliconia was anxious to sell the house and so it was necessary to keep everything spick-and-span at all times. Processions of estate agents brought wealthy clients who in the main, appeared to be Mafia *oilygarchs*.

Through the open window I heard laughter as I repainted the lines on the tennis court. I realised that Michelle had found some gem of comedy in my tale of law, order, handcuffs and sperm. As the day wore on I heard several more guffaws and shrieks. I must admit I was becoming a little concerned. When I'd tidied the bulrushes around the lake, I went indoors to find Michelle playing cuckoo clock coffee with her machine. I waited for her to speak.

"Oscar—we need to do something with the sex," she said.

"Really?" I said, loosening my belt in readiness.

"Really. Look I love the story but a woman sees sex differently from a man. It's not a matter of plumbing and fluid dynamics."

"Why didn't anyone ever tell me? Give me an example."

She picked up the manuscript and read out a section which she had highlighted in green.

"He felt the pumping hydraulic pressure of his erection. His sphincter valves had closed and the sinuses of his penis were bursting for release."

"What's wrong with that. I'm trying to explain the physics of love."

"OK—here's another one. 'She knew she was over lubricated but had no care. His saliva had mixed with her body fluid as his tongue stimulated her flap covered nerve endings."

"I suppose it is a little matter of fact," I conceded.

"And then there's the clothing and accessory issues," she said.

"Such as what?"

"Very few women carry a thirteen millimetre ring spanner in their handbag for instance."

"She needed it to tighten up one her lover boy's nuts but I take your point.

So, what's wrong with her clothes?"

"Blue and green? Black knickers under white cotton trousers? A tartan mini kilt with a tangerine chequered bomber jacket?"

"I want her to stand out—you know be ahead of the style curve,"

"She'd be arrested by the fashion cops Oscar."

"So, it's just the sex and the wardrobe stuff. None of that matters to me when I read a book. What matters to me is saving the submarine."

"Women notice this detail and sure don't want any hydraulic sinuses in the bedroom. The cars, buses, aeroplanes, violence, guns, crashes and boxing are great. It's obvious you've been in police cells a few times because the cop action seems real."

I had a sudden brainwave.

"Michelle—I appoint you sex and fashion editor. I'd like you to fix up all these issues."

"I think that's a brilliant plan Oscar."

"When can you start?"

"I'm on it. Give me a week."

It was an interesting week. Most days Michelle would read me one of her upgraded sex scenes and it was so disturbing that we had to lie down. I had to admit that the rock-hard unrelenting strength of man is more seductive than his hydraulically closed non-return penis valves. For those of us in the pumping professions it is sometimes difficult to escape into the abstraction of pure erotic love.

Also, a rejection letter had arrived from Blabber and Blabber the posh Bloomsbury publishers. I had sent them my collected poems as a kind of farewell to my life as a poet. I had provided a covering letter outlining my life as an artist and drainage specialist in case they wanted to provide a press release on the discovery of a genius or needed any gulley sucking. A wonderfully kind gentlemen wrote to me personally to say that my poetry was entirely without merit. However, he found my covering letter so entertaining he would be prepared to publish my collected letters if I continued to write to him. He added that they would no longer accept my unsolicited submissions. This was the pinnacle of my career in poetry. I was in contact with the gods who published Ted Hughes, Sylvia Plath and T.S. Eliot. I wrote back immediately to thank them for their encouragement. I assured them that in a life of disappointment and failure, they had offered me a beacon in the darkness. I wrote them my final ever poem.

Unsolicited Submissions
I know you never asked me to,
But I give in.

As far as I know this work remains on file somewhere in Bloomsbury Bibliotheque, Great Russell Street, awaiting my posthumous fame. I have asked the executors of my estate to offer Blabber and Blabber exclusive access to my literary legacy.

At last the day came when Michelle had written and read to me all the sexy girlie handbag and posh frock rubbish in the book. Drained and exhausted by her erotic readings, I stood at the post office counter to despatch our masterpiece to the New York offices of *Honeysuck Inferno*. When it had gone I felt a surge of sadness. My literary nest was empty. My professional life as taxi driver provided an adequate income.

It was 2011 and the world was changing. So-shallow media was metamorphosing into life itself. This was the virtual non-existent world where people were beginning to live their real lives. In August 2010, Amazon launched the Kindle e-reader in the UK after it's blazing success in the USA since 2007. Nothing would ever be the same again. In October 2011 I read a feature in the New York Times which opened:
Amazon.com has taught readers that they do not need bookstores. Now it is encouraging writers to cast aside their publishers.

This was the beginning of a new world. From this moment on, there needed to be nothing between the writers and the readers. In conventional publishing houses there was alarm, outrage and panic. Since the creation of the printing press, these

guys had acted as gatekeepers. They built a few star authors and convinced the world that only these few individuals, selected by them as the cream, were capable of writing a book. Also, they had created an orthodoxy around what was good and bad. They told their stars what to write and served their audience a regulation product. Suddenly the mob were at the door. People with sexual fantasies about goats would be writing science fiction where getting horny had a whole new galaxy of meaning. This was to be the Klondike and the first European foot on American soil all rolled into one.

At the same time so-shallow media lifted off. People on posh BBC Radio 4 started to be introduced as the blogger or the online journalist. It is not the function of this book to detail the rise of this phenomenon. There are many specialist histories for those who wish to read more. YouTube had launched in 2005 and iTunes in 2001. The technologies had been out there for a while. What it all added up to for the writer was that you could bring out your own book and Amazon would sell it digitally to their customers.

Comrades, brothers of the qwerty quirks, let's talk just between ourselves as insiders and artists. If you weren't there you cannot imagine the impact that these events had on the publishing world. For many—indeed, thousands, these were life changing days. Many writers of genius who had been too risky for the conservative editors, were loosed from their cages. Hundreds of thousands of regular wannabes poured through the hole in the dam, smashing the lowland valleys with mud slides of variable quality. It was a gold rush wild-west saloon fight with the sheriff tending his back-yard beans. The big publishers looked on in horror but could do nothing. As more prospectors charged into town, more and more merchants of shovels and mules showed up with self-help snake oil. Every priest and guru set up a church, every whore dropped her drawers and grabbed your wallet.

Amazon was a tight tribe who had lived on this territory for many summers. They watched the chaos, deciding when to reel it all in. In their quivers they carried their poison-tipped algorithms. By setting free the stampede they had brought to heel the chiefs of the other tribes. Big Chief Bezos now ruled the plains. The big guys protested, even tried not to sell their books on Amazon. It was useless to resist outright. It was time for a powwow.

Since that time much has changed. As an independent writer you are now a voice among millions yet the only show in town for you is Amazon, although as this book goes to press things are changing again. We are at the pre-dawn of the new High Street—the digital High Street of independent shops. All the same as of today, you can get your book out there, but getting the Amazon algorithms to line up to get anyone see your book is tough and getting tougher all the time. The big publishers have regrouped, merged a little and still have control of the few book shops that remain. They also have deals with Amazon on price and visibility that you cannot get. Five or six years ago I would have said there was no point in trying to chase a conventional deal. Today the question is far more difficult. The fact is that writing the book is the inevitable part—rather like giving birth. It's the next twenty something years of servicing an evolving product that's tough—and indeed optional. If you just want that book in your hand, step up and claim your prize. If you want a MONEY-MAKING best-seller or best-selling series, put this book down for a while. Get a degree in business studies, internet marketing and the science of algorithms.

As we awaited the reply from *Honeysuck,* we were learning about this new universe of possibilities. There was no shortage of advice and we busied ourselves with blogs, web sites and joining online groups. We needed to build our platform and presence but not identify ourselves. I knew that if I were to put my head over the parapet, Betty Black would shame and smear me. Michelle simply wanted to protect her children.

A letter had arrived from New York. A lifetime of rejection and mockery from above had prepared me for the worst. The text was simple. They had read the first three chapters and wanted to see the whole manuscript. That moment seemed almost like a success somewhere south of the Nobel prize but well north of an Olympic gold medal. And I was only fifty-seven. I was a little concerned about fame and wealth coming to me too young but posted off the complete book. By this time, I had learned a lot more about the business. I knew that my story was nothing like anything produced by *Honeysuck Inferno*. I figured there was an outside chance of an editor going maverick but I doubted it. In the meantime, I sent the first chapters to suitable agents selected from the hallowed pages of the *Scribes and Thespians Almanac*. Over the next few months all of them rejected me or claimed not to be accepting new clients.

Siliconia was still selling the house. Our estate agents, Liarsby and Bragg, brought a variety of clients to the door. It was one afternoon that I found a group of about twenty people wandering in the grounds. I kissed Michelle and left her unclothed on the pheasant food sacking in my game-keeper's hut. A large turbaned male seemed familiar. We regarded each other. I wondered if he recalled having marched me to the bank in order to take all my money.

"I know you," he said, poking me in the chest.

"And I know you. Will you kindly leave my estate?"

"Your estate—a loser like you?"

A crowd of children, grandmothers and affable plump guys in dark suits and turbans had gathered around me.

"Yes, all mine. If you remember you left me with ten pounds and eight pence. I placed a triple accumulator bet, won all three at five hundred to one, bought shares in the North Sea Bubble Bath Company and cashed in when they floated. If you'd been nicer to me I'd have cut you in."

"So, you're selling this place?"

"Yes—you know, trading up."

The rest of the family had formed a queue to shake my hand. Everyone loves a winner. I blessed their children with my golden hands. I knew this would be an every-day event once I hit the big time.

I noticed the estate agent rep' Jessica Wealthstone-Hart speaking urgently into her phone. Her accent was so posh and clipped that normally I had to ask Michelle to provide subtitles. Meanwhile the family had made towards a fleet of white Mercedes Cdi 220s.

Suddenly there was a confusion like a Bollywood crowd scene as they suddenly spring into dance mode.

"Look at my car. Look at my Mercedes!" yelled the big guy.

I looked. I knew. I knew.

A couple of half-bricks had hit the roof of one vehicle. Pebbles had dented other panels. There were a couple of cracked windscreens. The gates had been closed but evidently the attacker had improvised some artillery from distance.

"Must be someone with a grudge against you," I suggested.

"It's that woman you took as a child bride, who smashed the windows at the house. I know it is."

"She's been officially murdered. Contact Inspector Knight at Southleigh police. It's all nothing to do with me."

We stared each other down as the family began to drive away. Finally, he turned and went to his modified Mercedes.

"Looks like we've both got someone with attitude in our lives comrade," I said.

Jessica Wealthstone-Hart swept past me.

"You do *not* own this property. You're a pathetic total nobody. You wait until I speak to Connor Bryanston."

I shrugged. The children were forming up in Austrian costume and I still had a hot date in my game-keeper's hut.

24 CHAPTER TWENTY-FOUR

I needed to speak with Inspector Martina Knight. Could it be that Betty was back from wherever she'd been? Was this the nightmare all over again? The telephone in the hall was ringing. Michelle was at Kitchen Island, shredding organic passion fruit and mountain mist moistened Tibetan yams for a Pavlovian dog's breakfast. The phone never rang for me but I picked up.

"Yes?"

"It's Jessica Wealthstone-Hart from Liarsby and Bragg. My client has closed the deal."

"I thought Michelle was the client, anyway the price has gone up. He was nasty to me."

"He's paid the full asking price in cash—in short, you're out."

"A lot of that money is mine. I know you'll beg me, but I won't stay on as gamekeeper."

"It's funny you should say that. The deal only stands if you *don't* stay on."

The news of the sale pleased me. The place was enormous and I had never selected the role of groundsman. To find a house big enough for a family of seven children would be difficult. It was time for me to be assertive. All tortured and misunderstood artists exiled themselves in France. Once my genius became accepted as a cosmic constant like Stephen Fry and Clare Balding OBE, relocation to France would be an obvious chapter for the BBC documentary of my life. During our excursion to Paris, I had noted the huge size and modest prices of houses. It was clear to me that there was no other option but to embrace my Gallic artistic destiny.

"What about the children's education?" clucked mother hen.

"I had no education and look at me," I retorted.

"Exactly."

"Cruel but true. All the same what could be a better schooling than to be bilingual and knowing how you want your baguette baked? How many other six-year-olds can tell a *Côtes du Rhône* from a *Bordeaux* or an *Armagnac* from a *Cognac*?"

Michelle kissed my lips with the burning frenzy of a woman in a desirable *propertygasm*. She went to her computer and started to look at suitable chateaux under £50,000. I fell into a reverie of being a great but overlooked genius, hidden from the cruel world in my exiled turret.

A quick inventory of the children revealed that the two bearded males had left university several years before but had just stayed on because they liked the cuisine and the *lederhosen*. That only left five, a number too small to be statistically significant. The angelically beautiful grand pianist was about to take A-levels. The others were so entangled in the seaweed of changing educational currents that nobody knew if they were floating, swimming or drowning, including their teachers. Abandoning ship seemed no less rational than government educational policy. While I was waiting for the flowering of my own literary career, I would be able to *pomper la merde* as well as I could pump shit.

While these matters were in a state of semi-solid flux and packing of boxes, I realized that it had been several months since I had heard from *Honeysuck Inferno* in New York. I wrote them a letter and left it another month while I made sure I kept tabs on my own personal possessions. I folded my soup spoon and clock radio into a bin liner with my sleeping bag and I was done. It was several weeks later that I received a letter from America. This was a real soap opera cliché moment. With trembling hands, I tore open the envelope. The message was simple. *We cannot find your manuscript. The editor who was dealing with it has left.*

Once again my literary career had crashed. By the end of the day I'd prepared a replacement manuscript and posted it to New York. I'd only been writing for forty-five years, but I knew that every twist of fate was a step toward the greatness that destiny had pencilled ahead of me on the great spreadsheet of the universe.

Since my return from France I had resumed my daily ritual of attending the police station to sign on in the case of Regina v Sparrow. One evening I found the delectable Inspector Martina Knight waiting for me. I immediately explained to her that the story of the greatest ever police love affair starring her, had been temporarily lost in New York. She took the news with dignity and asked me to follow the perfumed trail of her loveliness to an interview room.

"Oscar—what did you know about Betty Black's past?" she began.

"Very little—she never struck me as the kind of person who would have had human parents."

"What charges would you wish to press against her if such a thing were possible?"

"None. You have to see her as an artist, passionate and wild. I'm sure you could see how a woman would lose the plot in her desire for me?"

"OK—here's the truth juice. She's barking bonkers but also a calculating crook. She embezzled a couple of a million quid from a wealthy client and high-tailed it to her place in Cyprus. She came back a few weeks ago but now she's slipped back out of the country."

"Why didn't you arrest her?"

"Her company don't want to splash the fact that their top barrister is a thief. By the way, she rolled in as a biker's old lady on the back of a brand-new Harley ridden by your one-time mate, Spike the bike."

"So, if anyone is going to give her trouble it's me?"

"That's about it. The other point is that you're off the hook and a free man. There's just one thing that's never made sense to me. On the floor in her burned out house in Great Western Drive there was half a toilet bowl. Was that anything you know about?"

Of course, I did know and it deeply hurt my sense of civic duty not to tell her.

"No idea—she was a bit avant-garde. It could have been a reflexive pun on Marcel Duchamp's iconic urinal statue. People often moan about modern art and the Turner prize but that work dates from 1916."

She tidied her papers and looked hard at me with a sigh.

"You'll never change will you?"

"I have changed. I have a wonderful woman in my life now and I'm on my way to wealth and fame."

"Just stay serious Oscar. As far as police is concerned, the case is closed. Here's your mobile phone."

And that was that. The road ahead was clear and nothing could hold me back. I celebrated by writing a short story for a newspaper competition. The Southern Express wanted Christmas content for their glossy weekend magazine. I penned a light little number about my experiences in a poultry factory, killing and plucking prime turkeys. The work was hard and cruel and many of the poor souls were exploited illegal labour. Also, it was pretty rough for the turkeys. I'd worked there when I had been laid off as a driver and had rent to pay. I sent off my manuscript and was astonished to receive a phone call from a very well-known American poetess called Carly Pollock, who was the writer-in-residence with the newspaper.

"Oscar—I've read you story. It's exceptional and brilliant."

"Did I win?" I asked.

"Well yes, but no. You see stories about blood, violence, cruelty, exploitation and poverty aren't what the weekend glossies are about."

"So, what happens now?"

"There's going to be prize winner's dinner with me and Pat Robertson We'd love you to be there."

"Is that Pat Robertson, poetry editor at Bullhorn Books and winner of the T.S. Eliot prize?"

"Yes, he's a personal friend."

I staggered to a chair. I was going to meet Pat Robertson and Carly Pollock. I would be among the intellectual greats. Too bad about the prize and the public acclaim. The universe had moved on but I was still only fifty-nine and it was simply a matter of time.

Comrades, fellow seekers of intellectual truth, you already know what I'm going to say don't you? Yes: in football you play to the whistle. In boxing you break when the ref says break and you stay down until a count of seven. You always give yourself the best chance. With my turkey death-story, I had failed to see

the unlikelihood of an editor who advertised Christmas dinners at exclusive restaurants and Marks and Spencer's turkey dinners for two, printing a story about breaking necks and torn arteries. Once again I had written the story I wanted to write. Once again I had failed in my objective of getting anyone to see it. The winning stories in this competition were about one of Santa's elves losing his booties and a girl who went to a Christmas fair and bought a magic toffee apple.

STUDY THE GAME. PLAY THAT EXACT GAME.

The great day of the dinner came. I sat opposite the two gods of literature. Me, a man dubbed by Blabber and Blabber as entirely worthless, a man rejected by every major publishing house over a forty-five-year period. Me, a shit-sucker writing about love in an abattoir, in the company of such greatness. To my left was the lady who had written about Santa's elves and to my right an octogenarian famous poet called Lizzie Hooper.

"What are you currently working on?" I asked in full obsequious-grovel mode.

She stared at me for a good minute, turned down the corners of her mouth and sucked in an Atlantic-sized spoonful of prawn cocktail. She looked me up and down while she chewed and fought hand to hand combat against her exhausted swallow reflex.

"Why do you ask?"

Her voice was deep and her accent somewhere north of the Queen.

"I don't know—I thought it might be the sort of thing one asks. Normally I drive taxis or sewage trucks."

A further minute of regurgitation and re-swallow passed.

"I'm writing *'From the Trenches'*."

"Ah yes, war poets, the Great War."

"Stupid man! They're my lesbian confessions. I felt it was the time to come out. Everyone in the poetry world knows my work in progress. *The Society of Poets* interviewed me last month. You must have seen it?"

"I understand lesbians—you and me, we go after the same stuff."

"What are you doing here? Are you actually one of us?" she asked.

"Of course, I'm the non-winner and the non-published."

Lizzie Hooper looked across at Carly Pollock who was feeding portions of battered garlic mushrooms into the open mouth of Pat Robertson as an act of poetic homage.

"This man hasn't read my feature in *Rhymesters Round-up*," she said.

"I think that's Oscar—our rough diamond," replied Carly Pollock with a wonderful poetic tone.

"I believe you're only half-right," said Lizzie Hooper.

God, it was thrilling to be at last among the razor-minded cream of intellectual society. Pat Robertson waved away an offered mushroom and spoke very directly to Carly Pollock in a broad northern accent.

"What's all this lass? Is this the horny-handed son of toil who barbarizes poultry yet finds a gem of beauty amongst the droppings in the cage?"

"Yes Pat, we couldn't get the capitalists to publish him."

"Ay—but you're still there, grovelling for the boss's shilling are thee not?"

"That's not fair Pat. I've got to earn a living."

"Nay lass—you've sold out to the oligarchs. You're lying on the soft cushions of capitalist complacency and silencing the voice of proletarian struggle."

Carly Pollock threw down a hand-battered gastro mushroom and stamped off in a poetic cataclysm.

"Ye can't censor a working man, Oscar, for the sake of gold. I'll never suck the rich man's sausage."

"A woodcutter wished for a sausage on his nose," said the elf story lady.

Here was my chance to impress.

"Originally a French story called *Les Souhaits Ridicules* by Charles Perrault," I said exhibiting my full cultural magnificence.

"Sheer pretension that doesn't become you. You've fucked up the whole show you vile man," said the wrinkled rhymester.

I ate my hand beer-battered ocean-caught prime cod fillet served with local minted garden peas, hand-cut triple-cooked artisan chips and an organic Caribbean tree-harvested lemon wedge in silence. I had used my time since Carly Pollock's phone call to buy and study all of her works and those of Pat Robertson.

"I've been reading all your work. I love *No Score At Half Time*. I imagine there'll be a few goals in the second half," I quipped.

"Ay lad, that's you and my mother have read it then," he replied fixing me with laser-like blue eyes.

"I thought it was wonderful," I said.

"Ah not me. It's immature crap but thanks for grovelling anyway."

"My pleasure."

I was on my way into the life of the mind. Ahead of me lay BBC Radio 3, 4, Melvyn Bragg or maybe Andrew Marr.

Since I had fractured the artistic universe, the gathering dissipated into the night without further stress or embarrassment. I knew that this had been a steep learning-curve for someone like me—someone from a different universe. All the same I had served the opening game and I was still on the court.

25 CHAPTER TWENTY-FIVE

The following morning there was a letter from New York. I found Michelle and asked her to perform a fanfare on her trombone. My urgent fingers fumbled for the letter within:

Dear Michelle,
 After careful consideration we have decided that your book is not for us. We very much enjoyed your story but criminality is never an element of Honeysuck Inferno stories. Also, we do not publish stories involving boxers. Thank you…

Michelle made a suitable deflating sound on her trombone. This was all very much as expected and in its way was a major step towards my eventual triumph. I was not downhearted.

Comrades—be never downhearted but also do not waste your time by serving rump steak to vegans—even though they may love it if you tell them it's syncopated aubergine roots. Think of books as cars for a minute. Once upon a time there had to be fins. Suddenly fins died out and in came the jelly mould. Before you write a line, focus on what is current. Look at book covers and how they evolve. Once you are tucked up with an editor or agent, they will tell you what to write. This is a process called *'may suggest revision'*. My third book in the *Milf In The Filth* series is about a regular black single-mum cop who gets caught up in international politics and ends up becoming

President of an African republic. Do you think a main-stream publisher is going to look at this story? Unlikely is it not? I sent the manuscript to a well-known and successful agent. Her reply was interesting:

Wow—great book Michelle. I've got a publisher who wants this story right now with just a couple of changes. We want the girl to be a white special code-breaking secret agent. Then we want her to ditch the politics angle and run off with a sexy black prince to Australia.

You can see that such a book would be rather different from my politically conscious satire/romance. Think of yourself as a tribal warrior trying to infiltrate another hostile tribe. Study the war paint, the design of their spears and the degree of acceptable gonad dangling under your loin cloth. Don't wear light blue at Old Trafford.
Of course, despite all discouragement, insult and failure, you may be a great writer. If like me, you braved decades of rejection but you're still scribbling, you comrade are my brother/sister or transitional re-arrangement. Fate had dropped into my hands the possibility of self-publishing. My dream was to produce powerful romance combined with police action. No one in the established publishing business wanted to know me. No more sucking up or grovelling. From now on it was me alone against the world but towards a better universe.

Before we could move to France we had to find a house in England to allow the children to complete exams. In the interim we had to leave Silicon Palais. We told the children that we would maintain their social status by still having the cuckoo clock coffee machine, organic carrots, avocado paninis and whole-wheat pasta. Since our artistic lives would soon become an utter fake, I told them they could concoct false holidays in Sumatra and ski trips in the Andes on so-shallow media so as not to be downgraded among their snobby peers. We decorated a bedroom wall in green screen background paint and posed all our boastful, beautiful life Facebook images in front of it. With a few backdrops we became hated globe-trotting champions of our friend groups. Our lunar holiday snaps with Lance Armstrong were a bridge too far when I mixed him up with Neil but hey, Neil Armstrong never did anything close to winning the Tour de France.

The day came when we moved to a tiny house in the nearby town of Rombury. Luckily there was a Waitrose supermarket nearby which stocked Fair Trade lemon grass. I spent several weeks welding bunk beds into triples with my Aldi home arc-welder and soon we were able to set to work on the creation of Michelle Mabelle. I'd never realised that Doctor Frankenstein was having so much fun. Firstly, we needed a photograph. We decided that we should be a sophisticated cool-looking blonde and chose a suitable model from the internet. Secondly, we needed a public personality to proclaim ourselves on so-shallow media among the cat videos. We set up a blog and launched a daily feature. In those days, everyone said you had to have a blog. Very soon blogging gurus began to sell self-help books on being a top best-selling blogger. Essentially you had to have some kind of honey trap. It was no good just writing about banal stuff like blocked sinks and your trip to ASDA. We decided that Michelle was a bawdy oversexed woman with a taste for British comedy seaside post cards and *Carry On* films. This was in order to accentuate our Britishness since it was clear that the main market for e-books was the USA. Once you have created an outrageous persona the daily dross of human life transforms into a farce of absurdity. This is because the daily dross of human life is fundamentally futile and absurd. We knew we'd touched some sort of limit when I decided to blog about my attempts to get small birds to use my televised nesting box. I headlined my feature "Is My Hole Too Small For My Tits?"

The outrage and unfriending from the Americans were such, that had we not already had a war of independence, one would have broken out.

The next important advice was to join online groups of writers. Over the following months I signed up to every possible band of partisans. There were thousands of guys and gals in the cyber-globe, all trying to get their stuff out there and then trying to get someone to read it or maybe even BUY it. We also joined blog syndicates where everyone pumped out all the other blogs. It wasn't long before the whole cerebral output of the world was a sausage string of blogs. Every writer in the world was trying to sell his/her book to every other writer. We soon began to see that in the long run we would have to involve the general public.

In the meantime, we developed our skills at book cover design. Here is everything we know about everything to do with Romance:

Naked men sell books to people who sexually desire naked men. You can never have too many abs or pecs. Despite everything in the Guardian or on the BBC, many women like men and like sex with men. This is our distilled experience over a decade. No political correctness can defeat the power of the buy button on Amazon. DICKS MEANZ CLICKS. Of course, one cannot expose the weapon itself but you can never ever lose by rattling your sabre in its bulging, straining sheath.

The day came when we launched *Punch-Up* on Amazon and a range of other platforms. It wasn't so much of a release as an escape. It just slithered out into the grey dawn of our innocence. In those days there were relatively few e-books and so without any parental interference, our baby began to sell. And people liked it. Before you get too excited remember this was 2011. The past is different country—they do algorithms differently there. The point was that one could have visibility and as I write this in 2018 with a string of best sellers behind me, it is a quantum difference of difficulty now to achieve the same thing.

Everything is a learning curve. Using what we had learned in publishing *Punch-Up,* we powered on to publish my own collection of poetry *Heaving A Brick.* It's worth knowing that no one buys poetry but zillions of people write it. All the same my little collection went to number one in the UK poetry chart on Amazon. My guess is that the highest daily sale was five copies. For what it's worth I was outselling the entire Blabber and Blabber list, Shakespeare, Seamus Heaney, Carly Pollock and Pat Robertson.

Although I had renounced poetry when Blabber and Blabber discarded me as entirely worthless, I continued to write and read poetry. There were several poets I'd noticed and admired on the internet and an idea formed in my mind to bring them together in an international anthology. During my sewage sucking life I had done a fair bit of stand-up poetry at open mic' events in pubs, cafes and glamorous C-list venues such as abandoned greyhound racing kennels. I came to see the true value of poetry was the voice of the poet. I coerced Michelle into helping me make an audio track of the selected artists. The resultant collection was *Ice Cream Headache* which once again hit the Amazon top ten. I will always be immensely grateful to the poets who joined us on that journey. So, there it was, a ground-breaking anthology with integrated audio track which none of the big guys had ever even contemplated. Michelle and I had produced it at home with less than £200 worth of specialist equipment. The only thing we needed to add was a music track to separate the different poets and to express their personalities. So how do you find someone to write and perform something like that? Luckily among the seven Von-Trapp children there was sufficient talent to eat the job. We dubbed our little publishing show *Mare and Stallion Media*. We're still up and running.

Everyone in every business, every crow in every tree is looking for opportunity. That is the nature of life. Anyone idly taking in the view should always know there's always a tiger in the bushes. Armed with our new tools we produced an audio book of my poetry collection *Heaving A Brick*. The Von-Trapp kids again did the music in return for extra portions of muesli and half an hour extra X-box access every other Thursday.

Exploit your children by giving them fabulous opportunities. If they ever get smart and use the word "royalties" in the house, wash their mouths out with soap.

26 CHAPTER TWENTY-SIX

With school exams out of the way it was time to move to France. From my three booze cruises to Cherbourg and my pedal to Paris I felt pretty much a citizen of the world. I was fluent in Edith Piaf and felt certain that plenty of people would want songs about suicide and failed love. Michelle knew far more of the place and had family in deep Provence. We knew we had to get south of the River Loire because everyone knows that the sun comes out as you cross the bridge at Nantes, heading for the Pyrenees. It was by chance that we stopped my overloaded London taxi in the small town of *Saint Saveloy Sur Frites* in the department of Charente-Maritime.

Being British one always feels obliged to seek a public toilet when one has need. These days, being more or less French, I'm scornful of such niceties. The toilet car park was crammed with British-registered brand-new Range Rovers and old posh Brit males in salmon-pink trousers with wee wee dribbles down the front. These were the ex-pats but I was looking for Charolais cow pats. We wandered into the town to buy a sandwich but the boulangerie was closed for lunch. Michelle spotted an estate agent's bureau and entered.

"Bonjour," she opened in perfect French."

"*Wee—bon jew-er*," answered a very attractive lady. If I hadn't known differently I would have placed her accent somewhere between Essex and Bordeaux—maybe somewhere like Dagenham."

"Anglaise?" I enquired.

"Yeah— 'ow can I help?"

"We need a house with at least four bedrooms for very little money," said Michelle. "My partner is a best-selling writer but he needs to live in squalor and poverty to maintain artistic authenticity."

"No worries me ol' cock sparrows—got just the drum wot you need."

Now this was real France. All nine of us climbed into the back of a Renault van and hurtled up a steep hill into the medieval quarter of the town. We stopped outside a substantial property with two savage dogs on chains guarding the crumbling wooden gates. I couldn't help but note three fridge freezer units on the litter and weed-strewn yard. One of the pit bulls looked ready to attack or choke to death as we opened the gates. A portly gentleman of about sixty wearing traditional peasant dress of blue overalls and baseball cap greeted us.

"Monsieur—you know why the tragedy of my life has happened?" he asked.

"I am acquainted with the tragedies of Edith Piaf and I have read Les Miserables," I replied in pure Franglais.

"Yes, then you understand Monsieur. It was her—yes that woman—she has left me for a young man. Yes, a young man you see. What would you do, Monsieur?"

"I'd sell my house quickly for any price and move on," I said, realising that I had absorbed horrible attitudes from working with Connor Bryanston and reading Donald Trump's book.

"Yes, I am thinking this also."

While Michelle kept the children away from the attack hounds, the gentleman took out a tin of rolling tobacco and rolled us both a very wet licked cigarette and pulled a half bottle of Cognac from his pocket.

"You, you my friend, are a labouring man of sorrow like me. Oh yes, we take a drink and have a smoke. You know the betrayal and horror of women—yes?"

"Of course, Monsieur. We are brothers under the scorched skin of anger and shame."

"Ah—yes, yes, you are a poet, mon ami."

We sat down on a pile of old wooden pallets, dragged hard on the cigarettes and swigged alternately from the bottle of brandy. It was only then I realized I didn't smoke. Michelle had flown into a frenzy of child-wiping following a couple of slips in slithery dog excrement. Finally, the estate agent led us into the house. A crowd of people were lounging in a smoke-filled salon. A couple of crawling children loomed and disappeared in the fog. Although drunk on Cognac and dizzy from my first-ever smoke, I noticed a central area of upright fridge freezers. The patron caught my unexpressed question.

"Someone here—one of my sons in laws I think—he fixes fridges. Monsieur, Madame—you must be excusing me. I have trouble of the *tripes* you see," said Monsieur as he sprinted to a small cupboard under the stairs. There followed some heart-rending groaning and evident release of something ghastly. The door re-opened on a windowless chamber containing a French stand-up toilet. The entire population of the house cried out in anguish as a cloud of ripe sulphur and methane hit their lungs.

"Monsieur, the body has its needs," he said.

"Mon ami—this business is my business," I replied with a Gallic shrug.

We toured the bare-boarded, filth-smeared, stinking, smoke-filled house. A piranha in a tank excited Michelle's curiosity.

"What does he eat?" she asked.

"There are many flies from the farm cows and the dog mess," answered the boss.

We completed the tour and finally scrambled back into the estate agent's Renault van.

"Wow—what a great place," I said to Michelle.

"What? It was a shithole. The whole place is vile."

"Potential—I'm a man of *merde*. Shit and heaving heavy weights are me. Give me two weeks alone here and then come back."

"No way—it's impossible." she said.

"What's that guy's name?" I asked the agent.

"*Monsieur Cacanard*."

Michelle went into a paroxysm of giggling. It seemed a very normal kind of name to me.

The agent dragged us around three other highly desirable properties, all smaller and all five times our budget. The following day we bought the house at a price of which I am ashamed even until this day. There followed days, weeks, months and years of toil to create Chateau Mabelle. There will never be a final tile or brick in this story.

26 CHAPTER TWENTY-SIX

While *Punch-Up* floundered on the ropes of the Amazon ring but stayed on its feet, I decided to write a series of short stories. I knew these would have little commercial potential. I had *Gizzards* the turkey farm story which had caused the poetic rift and the non-winning, non prize. I added *Prison Break, Glitter Ball Girlies, Cherubs* and *Striped Paint.* All of these stories related strongly to my own life in the labouring working class. We live in the shadow of identity politics, i.e. the idea that only a left-handed Eskimo can complain about a right-handed ice pick. *Glitter Ball Girlies* is a narrative of lesbian love. In my whole writing career, nothing has pleased me more than the critical praise given to this story.

During the production of the *Ice Cream Headache* audio book, Michelle and I had come up to speed with the techniques and opportunities in this business.

COMRADES—PIN YOUR EARS BACK COS THIS IS IMPORTANT. THERE IS MORE POTENTIAL IN AUDIO THAN THERE IS IN PURE BOOK PRODUCTION. IF YOU CAN'T READ YOUR OWN STUFF THERE ARE PLATFORMS LIKE ACX TO GIVE YOU EVERYTHING YOU NEED.

On the point of writing-style I would add that if from now on you imagine yourself reading your own book aloud, you will find

a magic fluency will brush your prose with its wings.

IF IT READS WELL OUT LOUD, IT READS WELL IN THE READER'S HEAD.

Amazon provides a platform called ACX—Audio Book Creation Exchange which matches up writers and narrators. If you can do your own stuff you double your potential profit. As this Self-Help Guide goes to press there will already be an audio edition, narrated by me. Always remember that your book is your voice. However, if you have a female protagonist it's tricky for a deep-voiced male sewage professional to tick all the boxes and maybe fulfil the expectations of the listener. At present the fabulously talented and endlessly patient burlesque actress Roberta Kalina is beginning to produce audio books of the Milf In The Filth series. She is the basque-wearing angel of the eardrum and bass.

Michelle and I decided to try the audio book business. If you think you just sit down and read aloud, then forget it. This is an acting job with a multitude of nuances and technical problems. You sniff, you make mistakes, you get a throat frog, you run out of air on a paragraph long sentence. You get numb, you get bored, you get drunk. AND YOU NEVER EVER QUITE GET WHAT YOU WANT. The playback is always a pale shadow of the genius you knew you were producing in the studio.

Life itself is an acting job. We imagine ourselves to be this or that tough-guy, sensitive artist, football fan or rarefied intellectual. The fact is most people are capable of being most things. We are held in roles and positions by the expectations of others, our timidity and as we age, our inertia. Sexually I'm a joyfully straight guy but I've never been in a position to have developed any other way. Love knows no frontiers and I'd say if I wanted a book on my desert island it would be Oscar Wilde's love letters to his lover Bosie—Lord Alfred Douglas, simply because they reflect so much the absurd poetic flower of love.

I decided to audition as narrator for a gay romance book called "The Knob and the Yob" by Austin Somerset and Antonia Trollope. I was delighted to get the part and this book

still sells and sells.

Would be authors: immerse yourself in the business. You can learn a lot about writing by doing an audio book for someone else. Take any chance to get involved in the great story that is showbiz. Michelle and I registered as film extras and worked on Midsomer Murders. Become that person, the ARTIST, the hack, the pro, the drinker from the fountain, trough and gutter of life.

While Michelle and I doodled in the general ambiance of the business, the great world beyond was changing and when I say the world, I mean Amazon. There are many opinions about Amazon and many gurus who act as priests, translators and readers of omens. Essentially, Amazon is the business. You cannot get anywhere commercially if you don't sell on Amazon. If you're a celebrity chef, footballer, Hollywood star or all three rolled into one, a mainstream publisher will get you into bookshops and put you on the front stand. If you're a poet or a literary writer forget it. You'll be in the back of the shop with the mop and bucket blocking your visibility. There's one guy I recommend for insights into Amazon. **David Gaughran and his Let's Get Digital books** are beyond price in terms of what you need to know. Therefore, I'm not going to waste your time with my pathetic observations. The fact is that Amazon bulldozed away all the old gatekeepers and allowed people like you and me to get their books out there. In the early days you could get visibility and sales. Now, you cannot and Amazon themselves are beginning to become gatekeepers. Increasingly their algorithms identify writers with commercial clout and then Amazon becomes their publisher. The algorithms then swing for those guys and the smaller fish get pushed more and more down the food chain. The principal book retailer in the world is now becoming the biggest publisher. This threatens the small guy but no less the big old-fashioned publishers. It could be that in ten years there will only be Amazon in the business and the embedded algorithms will decide what anyone will know or read for the rest of time. Top successful writers have to feed the machine. Many produce one novel per month, always the same genre always the same length, always the same terms of reference. If you love books and the quality of writing—be careful what you wish for if you want to be rich and famous as well. Some top *names* employ offices full of "assistants". Now, I wonder what they do all day?

The world was changing indeed. In December 2011 Amazon introduced KDP Select. The bottom line was that if you gave your book exclusively to Amazon, you could offer it for free to the world. And each free download counted as a sale and zoomed you up the charts. Then, when your book went back to normal price, you had that magic mushroom that changed all perceptions. You had **VISIBILITY.** You were the celebrity footballer on the front display table in the biggest book shop in the world. *Punch-Up* was a best-seller and people loved it. Amazon sent us money. Eighty thousand people grabbed a copy of our book. You could almost have thought we'd cracked it. Guess what—nothing ever stays the same. A little tweak of the algorithms and we were gone into the mud and the pond-life of people like Emile Zola, Aldous Huxley and Joseph Conrad. Gone—Invisible.

Although every one of our books since then has received the best-seller tag, nothing has ever matched that success. If you can imagine my consternation at being a best-seller, just imagine how it looked to guys like *Honeysuck* who had rejected me and countless thousands of others who didn't produce absolutely the required product. Even worse, those miserable readers loved these new wild books that stretched the envelope. **AND WHO COMPETED ON PRICE.** Amazon had those big fat guys by the short hairs and a peasant army of DIY serfs to chase them away forever. It wouldn't be long until the empire of traditional publishing struck back but that's another story.

Stop Press. Over the past year more and more platforms are becoming available to independent writers to sell direct online. Now you can publish, package and sell from your own web site. I'm watching this to see how it develops but it's tempting to scoop the whole book price for myself. All the same—am I a writer or not? A writer is someone who writes not someone who analyses sales results and sets up marketing pixels or whatever these guys do. I am the luckiest writer alive because I have a full-time tireless workmate. If you haven't—it's tough.

28 CHAPTER TWENTY-EIGHT

Having a best-selling book, a blog, a Facebook page, a website, a Twitter account, an Amazon author platform, a big mailing list and membership of online writers' groups affects your life. You start to smell of the same tribe, you roll in the same dung and urinate on the same lamp posts. The band of writers always reminded me of a pack of hounds, joyfully sniffing each other's bottoms but always glancing back at the guys on the horses and always aware of who has the whips. People start to talk to you about *The Craft* and your *characterisation*. You get letters from fans demanding to know what happened beyond the finishing point of your story. You get brilliant reviews from people who must be in touch with your mother for instructions from beyond the grave. You get twisted troll reviews that leave you afraid to go under bridges or to Scandinavia. You get invited to attend seminars and meetings of inner circles. I'll repeat that in case you didn't get the implications.

Yes, real live people want your real live body to appear physically in their presence.

This is the moment where the U-boat commander spots the destroyer closing at 194 degrees, range 5,000, speed *zu schnell. Achtung*—dive dive dive! Virtual *Michelle Mabelle* is a cool sophisticated lady purchased on the internet. Whilst the flesh Michelle is a creature of unassailable beauty, she *does not* resemble her public picture.

We stared at the e-mail. It was a warm invitation to attend the most prestigious group of romantic writers on the planet—*Biceps and Bodices*. A week-end meeting of the high council and regular members was to be held at a country house on the outskirts of Chipping-Sodbury in the County of Gloucestershire. There was to be a book fair, workshops with top advisors, lectures, readings, a gala dinner dance and as a grand finale, the induction of new members following a popular vote. Membership of these guys could be life changing. They networked with publishers and agents, they had the inside track on what was hot and what was not. They'd been the first guys to surf the *Vampire* wave and known exactly the point to wipe out and go *Billionaire handcuffs*. Most members had ten books or more in their portfolio. We were pygmies in the land of giants.

"I can't do it," said Michelle.

"You're so selfish—at least you've got the female plumbing job," I retorted with an enigmatic flare of my Latin nostrils.

"I don't write all the books."

"You do the clothes, the sex, the romance story line and the handbag contents. You ban the all the oily lesbian massage scenes I write and you do all the marketing, newsletters, promos and blogs. I do the fights, car chases, occasional submarine warfare tactics and the penile ejaculations. We're a team."

"Well, what about my face? That photo isn't me."

"No one will notice. You could tell them our next book is so hot it caught fire and you've had cosmetic surgery."

"The answer is, No."

"So, we can go no further. No one turns down *Biceps and Bodices*."

"Look, I accept we work as a team on the books. How am I, how are *we* going to explain the picture?"

"I never thought I'd say this but the truth sometimes works. You didn't want your kids to be reviled at the ballet class for having a porno-mum. I couldn't show out cos I had a mad stalker."

"Maybe they'd understand."

"Sure they will. They're fantasists—they make stuff up. They don't leave the house without a fictional smouldering desire in their longing follicles."

It was a wet Friday afternoon as we pulled into the car park of Bedmaster Grange, the stately home of the Duke of Cheddar. A liveried butler-cum-bouncer met us inside the grand doors. He stood at a lectern with his bare tattooed arms crossed. He had a list of names with photographs. I grabbed Michelle's wrist as she tried to bolt.

"Name?"

"You look like a Stud or Dirk," I said, playing for time.

"Your name? My name is Kevin."

"Ah, *je comprends*. Michelle Mabelle and I am *'er sexy lovair boy*"

"You are French?"

"Of course."

"You drove in with a London taxi?"

"*I saw a man in zee parking wiz a Citroen, zee English are very strange also.*"

"It's not the same photo," said Kevin.

"*We have different lenses. In France we have always our own national systems designed to be incompatible wiz zee rest of zee world.*"

He smiled while I pointed to the name *Mabelle*. He ticked it off and handed us identity badges and the keys to the Partridge Suite. We took the lift and threw ourselves with lustful abandon on the four-poster bed. Michelle drew the heavy hunting scene curtains and buried her beautiful face in her hands.

"I just want to hide in here. I'm an electronics engineer with a career in marketing."

"Would you ask an elderly sewage operative and eleven plus and literary reject to embrace the perfumed world of romance alone?"

"Fundamentally—yes. But I love you."

Poor woman—she had given her heart to one so unworthy.

"Leave it to me, I'll do the talking," I said.

Dinner was at 7.30 in the grand gilt-mirrored and chandeliered dining room. I gasped to see that we were seated with Harriet Sidebottom, famous author of the *Riding Crop Romp* series. Even worse was Cordelia Canestan, a lady from the Frills and Spoons stable with over two hundred Edwardian moustache-twirlers in her portfolio.

Michelle had dressed in a gorgeous midnight-blue ball gown and had made me wear a dinner jacket and bow tie. We looked underdressed. As we made our way trembling to the table, an excited lady wearing a 1920's style flapper feathered headdress stopped us.

"Excuse me—do you by any chance know Michelle Mabelle?"

"Yes," I began.

"Thank god. I'm Tamara Strangelove, president of the internal council. Everyone is so excited to meet her but we can't recognise her from the photographs. To be honest she looks so cool and sophisto we're terrified of her. They say she's got nine children, plays the trombone with the London Symphony Orchestra and ran off to France with some kind of refuse collector."

"That refuse guy is pretty cool," I said. "What's so hot about Michelle Mabelle?"

"My dear—it's those ghastly working-class stories about lesbians, criminals and abattoirs. Some say it's the next big wave."

"Like Fifty Shades of Grunge?"

"Wow—yes that's an idea but, I wonder—could you come with me and point her out?"

"I'd love to—but she's right here."

Tamara Strangelove stared at Michelle who was gazing blankly at a distant Sodom in the hope of turning into a pillar of salt.

"This is Michelle?"

"Yes, that sour stringy old bird in the photo was just to disguise her true beauty. A lot of people get nervous around Michelle because of her ample loveliness."

"So, she's not a super-sophisticated mother of nine trombone virtuoso?"

"She used to have a kitchen island and it's true about the trombone and the bin man."

"But that's not her picture?"

"No," said Michelle. "I didn't want my friends and neighbours to know I write about multiple orgasms during prolonged oral contact with sun-bronzed Adonis-types."

"Wow, yes I love lots of that myself, but lesbian abattoir looks far more natural to you," said Tamara.

I was beginning to like her. Suddenly she grasped Michelle's hand and led her to the centre of the dance floor. She picked up a microphone from a raised stage.

"Ladies and our one gentleman, please before we eat I have something really exciting to tell you. At my side is the real Michelle Mabelle. The sour superior hag in her photo was a clerical error. You can all stop searching for her and look forward to getting the inside track on gay abattoir romance. Yo! Right on. Let's chew some red meat gals."

Michelle gave a *tah-dah* circus wave and re-joined me.

"You're a total star," I said.

She shot me the glance of a woman who had suddenly realised that once you fully embrace fantasy, the world of the honest innocents lies at your feet.

Our large table was circular. Either side of Cordelia Canestan were two far younger ladies, both of whom clutched reporter-style notebooks. When Cordelia said one word, they scribbled ten. Neither of them seemed keen to chat and both wore identical porn-star spectacles. Cordelia Canestan herself looked us up and down and then looked away. I turned my attention to Harriet Sidebottom. She was a pale-skinned woman with such heavy dark eye make-up that she looked like a panda in an oversized frock. Luckily I had read a few of her *Riding Crop Romps* and had found them quite arousing.

"I'm a big fan of your romps—do you ride yourself?"

"Are you asking me if I gain stimulation with my legs spread by a big beast?" she replied in a *conspirational* tone, raising an eyebrow.

Just for once in my life I was lost for words.

"I was wondering if you ride yourself?"

"Well, we've all been there my boy. And you want to know if the pressure of the saddle is pleasurable."

"I've had a disturbing moment on my Raleigh Chopper," I said.

"Many men read my books out of a naughty boy interest in the private intimacies of women."

"Well, to be honest I've only ever glanced at the covers."

I left her to her naughty boys and watched the arrival of a voluptuous woman with a rounded body wrapped in a red dress. A large bow was tied around her waist, giving her the ambiance of Nigella Lawson looking out from a delicious Easter egg. She had two female companions who swept her along as if she were a newly-fertilised queen bee seeking her rightful place in the hive.

"Everyone—I'm Philomena Fish of Page and Turner Associates. This is Miranda Moxton—author of one hundred and eighty romances and non-fiction titles including The *Menopause Diaries, Beyond The Grind Of Love, Your Needs: His Prostate*, and of course, *Requiem For An Ovary*."

The speaker was a woman of about thirty with severely cut hair. The other companion was a kind looking woman who performed tasks such as pouring water and adjusting Ms. Moxton's hair.

"I've read all you books," said Michelle.

"And you are?" said Philomena Fish.

"And you are?" replied Michelle with a surprising spike in her tone.

"I'm Miranda's agent. Last year she produced fourteen historicals, a paranormal and three inspirationals."

I began to see that the queen bee metaphor was scarily apposite. The poor woman was a highly managed phenomenon of literary egg-laying. I glanced across at Cordelia Canestan. She was in hard discussion with her two assistants and clearly not impressed by anyone so far presented. On the other hand, I was humbled to be among such company. When Amanda Fish of Page and Turner, the world's greatest literary agency spoke to me I fought to control my fifty-nine-year-old heartbeat.

"What do you do?"

"Some say I'm a poet. In fact, I'm Oscar Sparrow, the Poet Lorry-Park."

"Poetry's boring shit but no one wants to admit it," she said. "And who's that with you?"

"She's Michelle Mabelle," said Michelle.

I could tell that Michelle and Ms. Fish would struggle to form a friendship as is often the way with ladies.

"Yah—that lesbian chicken-killing stuff."

"No, you're wrong. There are no lesbians in the chicken shed. The lesbians are in a sanitary supplies warehouse," I said.

"Yah—there's a few people wound up about it but that stuff's going nowhere. We couldn't give it away."

In the meantime, Michelle had struck up a rapport with Miranda who spoke in a glorious rural Chipping Sodbury accent.

"I heard you had nine children."

"Only seven—how about you?"

"Just the five."

"But how do you write all those books?"

"It's difficult but the ideas just come all the time, I can't stop them. I look up from my desk to breast feed the baby and I find I'm finishing another book. By the time the baby's asleep again I'm ten chapters in to my next."

"Do you type during the feed? Do you plonk the baby on the desk, latch on the nipple and hit the keys?"

Philomena Fish held up her hand in a traffic cop gesture.

"Miranda can't discuss her artistic process. She has four television appearances this week and you can tune in."

Our final tablemate had arrived. She was a lovely sunny faced woman in a hippy-style long dress. She had a tall willowy frame and a loud laugh.

"Bloody hell, I'm in with the big boys here. I'm Rachel Woods."

"You do TV sit coms?" said Michelle.

"Wow! You're that lesbian abattoir writer. I've been wondering whether there's anything there for a comedy series on the box."

"I'm more anxious to develop my romance style."

"Everyone's flogging romance. A lot of publishers only want thrillers."

Cordelia Canestan inflated herself and spoke with a loud school head-teacher voice.

"What? What? Romance is all there is at the heart of fiction." Her two gill cleaner fish went into a notebook frenzy. "My publishers need more romance than there is talent to write it. I have just completed my seven hundredth title."

"They didn't want mine," I said, realising that I'd forgotten my role.

"I said talent man. Any buffoon can bang words down on a page."

I declined to involve myself further and turned to Harriet Sidebottom.

"So, does the riding stimulate your creative imagination?"

She rewarded me with a warm smile and a pat on my arm.

"I knew straight away you were a naughty boy. As it goes, I've got a cowboy horned saddle—,"

Comrades, my companions along this rocky trail, we have journeyed far together. We began without a book and without

any knowledge of the business. We were non-people in our own estimation. Now we find ourselves in the foothills of the great mountains. For many this will be far enough and comrades, I love you and salute you.

From now on the air gets thinner and the food scarcer. If you set out with the ambition to write and publish a book—any book—the tools are there to give you that achievement. You will be able to invite folk to dinner and show them the book. You'll impress them and they will all tell you that everyone they've ever met told them that they themselves should write a book. I advise all writers self-publishing to use the print copy production facility. Few people will buy your paper copy but you'll have copies to sign and use for prizes, sell at book fairs etc if you now climb on further.

We've been looking at those first steps into the hallowed halls of the greats. OK—you've written a book. Most people now will shrug and say, "So what?" With one book, you are a bacterium in the gut of the elephant. When you meet these multi-best-seller writers you realise why people pay half their week's wages to watch premiership football. These guys are total pros. Some of them are lovely, lovely people. Some are arrogant and dismissive. On sunny days they're not at the beach, they're not at the match, they're not scuba diving for pearls in the Caribbean. A writer is someone who writes.

This is the totally true story of a sewage tanker driver who became the best-selling romantic novelist Michelle Mabelle. However, all of the success is entirely the work of my partner Michelle. She sorts out the sex, clothes, handbags and works tirelessly on the marketing of the product. She removes all reference to lesbian massage. She is an experienced marketing professional. She edits and advises at every stage of writing the stories. I could not do this on my own.

OK—there's a few of you still with me. We're apprentice floor sweepers in the golden tower of LOVE production. Never look up to see the top of the building. It will always be in the clouds.

29 CHAPTER TWENTY-NINE

Most people are familiar with the Oscars, the Baftas and The Emmys. The show-biz world loves awards and there is something validating about the acknowledgement or even admiration of one's peers. After a wine-drenched dinner there were the *Beebees*, the cherished medals awarded by *Biceps and Bodices*. First up was the adorable Miranda Moxton, voted as *Author of the Year* for her twenty-part Regency period, bad-boy billionaire box set, *Tatts, Lats and Spats*.

In second place was a splendid woman in a shocking-pink evening dress and black feather boa who took the silver medal with her religious fantasy feline trilogy *Litter Tray Litanies*.

Cordelia Canestan took the Purple Rose prize for her inspirational box set collection *Golden Tears In The Sunset of Sorrow*.

There followed a list of more technical awards. A lovely red-haired woman won the *Best Blurb* engraved glass scroll, while the *Pumped-Up Torso Cover* prize was won by a lady of about ninety. Finally, it was cabaret time. Tamara Strangelove spread her hands wide.

"I know you want them girls. I know you love it. Put your hands together for the nation's hottest cover boys—the sexy, the rock hard, the six-pack of the gods, the dukes of dicks, the inspired by literature—it's the one and only *Lords of the Flies*."

A group of eight honed and oiled hunks in tight denim shorts and bow ties sprang onto the dance floor, grinding and self-massaging around the falsely coy Tamara. She stroked their glistening lats while they circled with lascivious expressions. Rock music wailed as drunken romantic ladies burst free from their chains, got up and went to the dance floor. Michelle and I had no option but to join in. Soon she was mesmerized by a tight-bottomed lifeguard-type who was unbuttoning his waistband. I found myself with the ninety-year-old lady who had won the cover prize. She shimmied and pointed to my trouser belt.

"I'm fifty-nine," I said.

"You're nearly old enough mate—I won't say nuffink."

Sometimes it's hard to make a woman happy. During a lifetime at the shrine of Venus, I'd tried with chocolates, flowers, jewellery and poems. I believe a flash of my threadbare Y-fronts achieved as much female happiness in that moment as I had ever achieved.

Comrades, we are artists because it brings pleasure. When you get the chance display your art.

The entertainers melted away, taking with them a couple of romantic ladies. Michelle was relaxed and happy. It had been a great night and I loved these guys. Tomorrow was another day.

The day began with a book fair. If you join the ranks of the pros, these fairs are a peculiar rite of passage. No one really likes them but no one ever says so. The function of them in my opinion is the networking opportunity they provide. I think of them as a murmuration of starlings or the evening chorus in a rookery. As far as selling books, I'd rather go door to door with encyclopedias in a suitcase.

We assembled in an empty retail unit on the outskirts of Chipping-Sodbury. Michelle and I set out our small display. On the adjoining table was a guy who did spiritual healing. I noticed that he excited more attention than the straightforward hardcore romantics. The tradition at these fairs is that you swap books with other authors in the classic I'll show you mine if you show me yours routine. I enjoy this and have often used it as a tactic in my personal life. I approached the healer with a copy of *Punch-Up* and a priceless signed first edition of my collected poems. He glanced at them and shook his head.

"Not my thing I'm afraid—I'm more a man of the spirit your see," he said.

He was a middle-aged guy with a two-strand comb-over, a hand-knitted tank top and open sandals worn with a black suit. I shrugged and looked at his books one of which was entitled *Reiki Spiky—a self-help guide to spiritual tough love.*

"Are you aware of Guru Gung Ho Tsunami Bagwash?" he asked.

"Does he play inside right for Spurs?"

"I'm afraid he's crossed to the other side," said the writer with a sad voice.

"What? Surely not Arsenal?"

"What are these words? These aren't terms of the spirit."

I noticed that several females had gathered around his table. He attended to a good number of sales and asked a senior lady with a Tesco carrier bag full of leeks to sit on a plain wooden chair in the centre of the room. He moved behind her and hovered his hands around her head like a baker kneading an invisible ball of dough.

"I'm seeing your aura. I'm feeling the inter cranial currents," he said.

"I feel it, I feel the force," said the woman.

The healer poured out an incantation of magical words.

"Whoa, Bhuna, Korma Chamelion, Rogan Josh, Whiplash Madras—whoa—feel the field, feel the amps and volts, feel the spark. Whoa—wallop!"

He sprang back as the aura-force hit him and made him stagger. The woman was twitching and groaning in such a way as to portray the ultimate pleasure. Slowly she regained her composure.

"The tension's gone. I'd been looking for release for over a month," she said.

Within ten minutes he'd sold all his books, packed up and sat at his table with a giant hot chicken tikka slice.

"That was one hell of a show mate," I said.

"It's not a circus. That was the revelation of the powers of the guru. I'm just the conduit."

"Do you have a day job?"

"I was a clerk at the gas company. I was made redundant eighteen years ago. I hit rock bottom, turned to drink, sex and gambling. I lost my marriage, my children and my home. I was wandering alone near Coventry when I met Gung Ho Tsunami Bagwash in a bus shelter where I was hoping to spend the night. He took me to his temple and taught me everything I know."

Comrades, sewage suction folk are not known for their spirituality. I will confess to some cynicism with regard to such powers. However, this guy sold books and I know that he believes totally in what he does and the healing he brings to others. The difference between a showman and a priest is so small that I don't think there is a difference. They are guys representing their goods in the most attractive and appealing way. As a writer you will struggle to get attention and its commercial cousin, VISIBILITY. I've come across brilliant writers and real show biz troupers performing karaoke and belting out rock ballads acapella. This is what I call the naked tight rope walk effect. If you happen to be naked at Niagara Falls and there happens to be a rope ask yourself how much you want to be a best-seller. Once you've thought, phone the TV companies and go for it. You're selling yourself as much as you're selling your book.

There's a certain self-consciousness about being a writer. You enter a tradition of craftsmanship and also social responsibility. Those vile plebs out there need *the book* to help them become civilized and worthy. Like the ancient Christians you are missionaries. There are prestigious literary festivals where the greats read their genius-laden texts to rooms full of acolytes. BBC Radio 4 send special correspondents to catch any gem of beauty or insight from the spouting lips of literature. The internal council of *Biceps and Bodices* formed part of this tradition. Therefore, on a wet Saturday afternoon, a band of writers formed up in a nearby shopping mall to take turns reading from their books while standing above the retail herd on an upturned milk crate. Clearly a large applauding crowd of literature starved peasants would form—wouldn't they?

I watched as a procession of ladies read chapters from their books. I noted that words like *breasts* and *knicker*s could draw in a few older males in raincoats, sometimes finding myself in a crowd of three. Poor Michelle battered on, detailing erotic boxing champ thrusts in a Parisian penthouse. When the PA system failed she continued with a loud hailer. My heart pounded as it was my turn to step up. I had decided to read from the *Ice Cream Headache* poetry anthology. I had an audience of one man with a howling dog. Every time there was a squeak of feedback from the loud hailer the poor beast leapt in pain.

"Poetry's boring shit mate, but no one wants to admit it," the owner called out in a broad Chipping Sodbury accent.

I completed my twenty-minute stint and staggered to the co-op off licence. I selected a budget litre of Merlot and sat down on the tiles, drinking from the bottle. Michelle joined me.

"You're not a proper genius until you've been humiliated and ignored," she said.

Half drunk, I kissed her with melting tenderness in the style of Ricardo di Napoli, oblivious of the shoppers, losing myself in the physical expression of emotional love. I was aware of applause and a crowd around us as we straightened our clothing and re-zipped. Michelle quickly opened a box of books. We sold the lot and were on our way back to Bedmaster Grange as we met the police running into the mall with drawn riot batons and buckets of water.

Comrades, you are never closer to victory than you are at the point of utter defeat. A writer is someone who writes. A writer is someone who gets pissed, tears it all up and writes all the next day with a headache.

At the evening reception, writers once again had the chance to give readings. My own cover story was that I was a romantic poet although I'd never been to the Lake District and sneezed at the sight of a daffodil. Everyone was tired, everyone wanted to let their face muscles sag into non-person, non-giving-a-fuck mode. I was the last performer.

"Ladies—I've met some brilliantly talented people and I feel humbled to be here. I'm probably the only sewage professional with a nibbled X-chromosome in the building. I want to read you a short piece about those times when things won't quite pump up—when you're trying to find that perfect form of words or catch the moment of a sunset. It keeps teasing you but droops before your eyes. This is my little poem in homage to all artists in that situation. It's called *Erectile Dysfunction*. Shamelessly I quothed my masterpiece.

*You would have thought
that by this time
of schism in the church of rhyme,
I would be through
with all the this and that
of what and thing—
already thrown with
the towel, the grammar
and the hat
in the ring.*

*Yet, still camping with intent
in the embers of the member's exclosure
I brake and clutch
at cliché straws
still blowing in the Dylan wind
erecting and correcting
the poem fallen in
the—Oh well, never mind—
but pumping up...
now here it comes,
just where I was just now
not quite
but almost very nearly was.*

*Please take this soft option
and never tell a soul
beyond this warm and crumpled page,
how much you know of me
or how it really was for you.*

There was laughter and genuine amusement as I read my little phallic ode. At the end there was applause—applause from the cream of romantic fiction writers. I'd come a long way to find myself at home. The crowning point of the day was when Tamara Strangelove, president of the internal council, announced that Michelle had been inducted into *Biceps and Bodices* as a full member. Although we'd never applied to join the *League of Love*

Writers' Guild, our acceptance here made that a certainty if we chose that path.

I noticed Michelle in deep conversation with a woman whom we had already learned was an agent. I kept myself aloof and poetic. I looked at the selection box of gorgeous women around me, wondering at how Michelle had cured me of my affliction of serial religious experiences at the shrine of Aphrodite. When we withdrew to our room she told me we'd received an offer from a mainstream publishing house. Now for sure, that was something to sleep on. We're still sleeping on it.

Although this is a self-help book, it is also a romance and a love story. Michelle and I had shared the load and the underwear.

"If I'm going to pose in your frilly knickers for the rest of my life, I'd want you as a wife. It's only fair. All I can do is offer you is equal access to my Y-fronts in return," I said.

"A Las Vegas Elvis wedding?" begged Michelle.

"As long as the king sings Edelweiss and you play the trombone."

A few months later we made the trip, complete with pink Cadillac and wind section.

Comrades, this is the end of the book in the sense that the story is over. This is a true story. Everything in this book happened but with different characters, different locations and in many cases fictional book titles. The central truth is that a male sewage tanker driver became a multiple best-selling female romance writer. I must qualify this by saying that Michelle does most of the work and shapes the books from the crude effluent of my sexually inventive imagination. I wish I could reveal who I am. To do such a thing would shatter the trust of my thousands of fans. In the gender-divided battlefield of modern society, Michelle Mabelle proves conclusively that men and women are not and should never be strangers or enemies to one another. Sexual desire and the passion of emotional love unite us. Joyfully naughty sexual fantasy and longing to release from loneliness and physical need, drive both male and female equally. Never let self-righteous duplicitous people of either or any sex spoil

your joy of uninhibited love and pleasure for their selfish political ends.

This is a story that will never end for any of us. The point at which we leave Michelle and Oscar was just the beginning of their publishing career. My latest release has just achieved the coveted Amazon best-seller tag. Every one of my Milf in the Filth stories has hit a number one target on Amazon.com. We are still independents with our own publishing business because I want to write my way and I'm a stubborn bastard. What drives me on is the joy I receive from my readers. That is worth more to me than money or maybe even life itself. If you've had another knock back today I know you're down. I'm sharing that moment with you comrade. Everything I'd ever submitted had been rejected, often with rudeness or superior intellectual disdain. Sometimes they were right. Understand this truth. Don't write simply from your heart, that's not enough. Write with your tears, your anger, your fear and your wickedness. If a sad scene doesn't leave you in tears, scrap it. If a sexy scene doesn't stimulate you, scrap it. This approach is my bond and my promise to my wonderful loyal fans. If you've read this far, you've got the guts of a pro. If you want to say hello and tell us your own journey we're there for you. If you want to know where to go next we've added some links. I know your struggle and you matter to me. When you're fighting off the bottom, life is often a painful rejection. That anger is your fuel. That insight into yourself is the core of your next fantastic character on the page. When you're as professional with the knocks as you are with the flattery, you're good to go as far as you want.

If you've come with me this far you're not going to be a winner. You are a winner! I offer you my defiantly defiled hand. I love you.

EPILOGUE

It is September 2019. Nothing stays the same. Darwinian evolution never encountered the beast of modern media or the shape-shifting power of Amazon algorithms. Many of you reading this will be authors or would be authors. UNESCO statistics indicate that somewhere between two and three million books are published every year. At one time the novel was like the saxophone before the electric guitar. We all know who won. Novelists compete against a mass of wonderful vibrant and exciting forms of entertainment. Just look around you on the train or aeroplane. Folks are watching Netflix box sets and YouTube videos. For sure there'll always be saxophones but kids won't be doing air sax in front of the mirror. The good news is that fiction has never been so popular and there's some fantastic guys out there putting the new media shows together. My own opinion is that the audio book will become the modern iteration of the novel. People still read books but you have to acknowledge that the novelist is just one voice shouting in a teeming crowd. Thousands of top-quality books are offered for free by authors trying to gain traction and visibility. It's tough to beat those guys on price.

We all know the old saying that the guys who got rich in the gold rush were the ones who sold shovels. It's a cliché and it's true. In the run-up to publishing this book I approached a range of literary agents. I took great trouble to follow all of their requirements and conditions as set out on their websites and in *The Scribes and Thespians Almanac.* Half of them did not reply. One of them wrote back within an hour saying I'd previously contacted him and he would have nothing to do with me. I had never ever dealt with him. All the rest sent short curt refusals. Within a few days I started to receive advertisements for writing courses from some of the people I had contacted. One outfit offered me courses on how to meet literary agents. Next they offered me week-end speed dating opportunities at special and expensive seminars where I could meet agents and *top* authors. When I checked out these superstars they were rated lower than me on Amazon. Every few days I receive messages from these *agents* telling me that some lucky soul has just gained a *publishing deal* following their attendance at courses run by them.

A few days ago, I came across offers from very well-known writers offering master classes to help me be as good and successful as them. Just today I received a special discount offer on a range of courses run by *The Scribes and Thespians Almanac*. Comrades, you must make your own judgements of such matters. The fact is you can publish yourself if you just want that book in your hand. Just make it the best book you can write. You know when that is because it's *your* book. My advice is to be aware of sharks in the water. Very aware. Highly prestigious *literary* addresses need not signify moral probity. It would be harsh of me to say that there those who pose as agents in order to scoop would-be authors as gullible students on their own courses on how to get an agent. Comrades you do not need these guys or to give them hundreds or even thousands of your pounds, euros or dollars. Now, there is a quantum universe between getting a book out there and getting any sort of sensible income from your writing. Getting a number one best-seller, even for a few hours is more about marketing than about the content of your book. There are independent authors who spend thousands of pounds on marketing. There are authors who spend big money on advertising their own courses on how to be as great as them. Like I say comrades, selling shovels can scoop you more than digging for gold.

The only reasons to write a book are because you love writing and you want to give a reader a great experience. If your ambition is for wealth and fame join the end of the X-Factor audition queue and take a good book to read… I recommend a Michelle Mabelle title.

Finally, let me say a few words about Amazon. Yes, it is a monopoly and it is popular to blame them for all the evils of the universe. Comrades, in the sweep of history all empires crumble. Amazon gave me and gives you the chance to get your book out there. The old elites formed an arrogant empire which wanted us all to believe that only a few humans were capable of producing a book. Those few would be chosen by them, often from their own social class and friend group. After decades of rejection I was able to publish books which thousands and thousands of people love to read. To Amazon it doesn't matter if ten million people sell one book each or one person sells ten million books. After all, we are all equal alone with our pen or keyboard. Many important politicos talk about social mobility these days. The old elites had no interest in the voice of the great mob of plebs. Self-publishing is the most powerful weapon ever issued to the peasant army. Let's grasp it comrades.

I am co-partner in my own publishing business. We have followed the successive waves of gurus and trends within the self-publishing business since it all began. We are still here.

THE END

A MESSAGE FROM OSCAR

Thank you for reading this story.

I hope you enjoyed it? If would be wonderful if you could post a review for me. Either drop me an email, to oscar@galloromano.co.uk, or post on this link:

https://smarturl.it/ReviewKnickers

I cannot compete with the big guys who employ complex machines and budgets to promote their titles, but your feedback helps other readers find my work and means so much to me. Thank you.

Hoping to share more with you in the very near future.

Regards,
Oscar

P.S. If you can identify the REAL names of my female-romance-writer alter-ego, Michelle Mabelle and the 'Milf in the Filth' book series, drop me an email oscar@galloromano.co.uk and I'll send you one of the books from the series for free as a reward!

FREE BOOKS FOR YOU…

If you enjoy my writing, why not keep up to date with my new releases, giveaways and competitions by joining my VIP Reader Group **'The Suck It Up Club'**?

I'll send you a copy of my short story 'Champions' as a welcome gift. Click the image or the link below, or use the QR code to join my club now:

https://smarturl.it/CoverSuckItUp

As a valued reader, you'll get exclusive freebies, special offers, goodies and giveaways, un-published extras and the chance to get pre-release editions of my new books before they go on general release. There might even be a chance for you to get your name (or one of your friends!) into my next book as a supporting character! **You just can't get this stuff anywhere else.**

I like to reach out several times each month with news and bargains, but don't worry, I won't bombard you and will never share your details. You may of course unsubscribe at any time.

MORE BOOKS BY OSCAR SPARROW

THE COVER UP

What could link a webcam girl, a cross-dressing police chief and an escaped ferret?

A British nation torn by Brexit staggers on. Frankie Ferret, a pre-school children's TV celebrity, escapes into sewers of London and surely is dead. The people unite in grief. Police Chiefs, counselors and politicos stand in tear-stained sincerity with the common people. Viktor Pinupskin of Russia offers a genetically modified bear cub with his own face as a substitute. Internet bots urge a vote and attempt to sway the masses. Chaos and panic threaten to destroy the economy.

Into the mix steps young police inspector, Crispin Bissel. His mission is to lead the search and target PR for the cops. His ex-girlfriend, Selena Fontesse, is a mature ex-webcam girl specializing in veggie porn. She has the looks and the bosom to comfort a people broken by sorrow.

Could love be re-kindled over an open drain? Could Frankie be alive? Could a billionaire, a hot air balloon, a pop star, and a staring messianic child, bring happiness back to a population in despair? And what if the big plans were to fail?

What if there were a cover up?

A deplorable basket-case of a book. All right-thinking people should be offended. Cross-dressing vegan cannibals will *love* this story. There's no safe space on campus when a ferret like Frankie gets into the pipes. A tender love story, an outrageous unfair satire, an exposé of the media-cult whirl in which we live, where news, fake news and spin are the currencies of coercion.

Buy this book and forgive yourself for laughing. It's not incorrect if you didn't mean to.

http://www.books2read.com/TheCoverUp

CHAMPIONS

A short story about a time when the colour of the jeans you wore defined your tribe.

https://smarturl.it/ChampionsSale

I THREW A STONE

https://smarturl.it/OscarStone

Available in e-book, print and audiobook formats. Poetry recorded by Oscar Sparrow with original music soundtrack.

FREEZE FRAME

https://smarturl.it/OscarFreeze

Available in e-book, print and audiobook formats. Poetry recorded by the poets themselves with original music composition leitmotifs.

HANDY RESOURCES FOR WRITERS AND SELF-PUBLISHERS

If you're planning to write or self-publish, here is a link to a page I've set up with a few resources that I've used and would recommend as great time-savers, easy to use or most professional.

Some are free, others are paid, many have a free starting level so you can try before you buy. I can only vouch for these tools from my own experience and there may of course be other tools that exist that are cheaper or more suited to your level of expertise.

I've hosted these on an external page so I can keep them up to date. (N.B. The links to some of these sites are affiliate links which means I will be paid a small finder's fee if you join up.)

Check out links here: **http://www.smarturl.it/PubResources**

Software tools
Author Websites
Image creation (ads/FB posts etc)
e-book creation tools
e-book hosting and delivery
Audiobook production, hosting & delivery
Print book hosting and production
Giveaway and competition hosting
Mailing list hosting.
Keyword Search
Landing page creation and management
Direct Sales Cart

Service Companies
Cover Design
Book formatting
Book promotion

Courses
Writing book descriptions
Self-Publishing skills
Book Advertising
Growing a mailing list

ABOUT OSCAR SPARROW

Oscar Sparrow was born in Winchester UK in 1949, apparently thanks to the American Marshal Aid program to re-build Europe after the war. As the colour red leached its way out of the map of the British Empire, Oscar attended a die-hard Church school designed to create noble savages to serve what was left of the savage Nobles. The Eleven Plus exam revealed that he could not even count to eleven and he became a mechanic, labourer, truck driver, boxer and poet.

He read Wordsworth and Ford Cortina manuals in a lorry cab near both Oxford and Cambridge universities. He married a kind forgiving woman who eventually forgave herself for that one big mistake. He has several wonderful children and hopes that one day they will all meet.

At the age of 25 he heard the music of Edith Piaf and learned to sing all her songs. A few years later he realised she was French and that he was an ugly swan not a beautiful duckling. The shock propelled him to London where he joined the Metropolitan Police. Car chases and riots followed but he did not take it personally. He spent his spare time touring the Art galleries, singing Piaf and learning Italian. Eventually, The Authorities fell for the con and gave him a desk job in the Art department of Interpol London at Scotland Yard.

One day a few years later, the lure of the wild swept him away to the roads of Europe as road gipsy trucker. His love of fried battered fish eventually drew him back to England where he drove sewage tankers and set up a taxi business.

FIND OSCAR SPARROW ON THE INTERNET

Blog: **https://oscarsparrow.wordpress.com/**

Twitter: **https://twitter.com/Oscar_Sparrow**

Facebook Fan Page:
https://www.facebook.com/TheTurdMan/

YouTube: **http://www.youtube.com/OscarSparrowWriter**

Instagram: **https://www.instagram.com/virtualbookcafe/**

BookBub:
https://www.bookbub.com/profile/OscarSparrow

Amazon Author Link:
http://www.smarturl.it/AmazonSparrow

PUBLISHER

This book was published by Gallo-Romano Media. For details of other books and authors or if you would like to submit your book for publishing:

Email: **contact@gallo-romano.co.uk**
Web: **http://www.gallo-romano.co.uk**

www.ingramcontent.com/pod-product-compliance
Lightning Source LLC
Chambersburg PA
CBHW021101080526
44587CB00010B/325